Jeanie Thomas Gould Lincoln

A Pretty Tory

A Romance of Partisan Warfare

Jeanie Thomas Gould Lincoln

A Pretty Tory
A Romance of Partisan Warfare

ISBN/EAN: 9783744673402

Printed in Europe, USA, Canada, Australia, Japan

Cover: Foto ©Thomas Meinert / pixelio.de

More available books at **www.hansebooks.com**

A Pretty Tory

Being a Romance of Partisan
Warfare during the War of Independence in the Provinces of Georgia and South Carolina, Relating
to Mistress Geraldine Moncriffe

By Jeanie Gould Lincoln
*Author of " Marjorie's Quest," " A Genuine Girl," " An
Unwilling Maid," etc., etc.*

Say, pretty Tory, coy as fair,
Of the King's colors be you 'ware,
When in those eyes of heaven's own hue
Reluctant smiles the rebel blue!

The Riverside Press

BOSTON AND NEW YORK
HOUGHTON, MIFFLIN AND COMPANY
The Riverside Press, Cambridge
1899

To G. G. L.

The story was planned in the Long Ago,
   With a merry jest and a smile,
But the heart we knew so loving and true,
   Has gone Beyond for awhile.

And now, on some leaf as you turn its page,
   If you trace an ideal fair,
You will see and know that the Long Ago
   Has been tenderly written there !

Washington, D. C., *August 23, 1899.*

CONTENTS

LIST OF ILLUSTRATIONS

A PRETTY TORY

CHAPTER I

A FAINT pink glow crept softly up on the horizon where the sky and water met off the Bay of Savannah, and the slight mist of a spring morning lifted slowly, disclosing the ships which lay at anchor near the city. Of these the most noticeable was His Majesty's ship Vigilant, that with her consort, the Phœnix, and two corvettes, having arrived in port the night before, was preparing to land the troops just ordered from old England upon the shores of her rebellious colonies.

Below decks, the men were busy packing their kits and making ready for disembarking as the sailors unswung the ship's boats from the davits. Then the roll sounded and the soldiers formed a line on deck, and their officers came up the companion-way, accompanied by the captain of the ship.

"I have to thank you for much courtesy, Captain Thornton," said Major Sefton, the officer in command. "You have made a long and tedious voyage seem short, and I shall surely report your kindness to Sir Henry Clinton."

" Duty, sir, duty," returned the British captain somewhat gruffly, "though I may add, pleasure also, in your case and that of your brother officers. I have never had a stouter set aboard my ship; I would rather land you at Southampton, however. These American rebels are a pestilent sort, and fight like devils; your men and you are too good to serve as targets for them."

" I think you reverse matters somewhat strangely, sir; we came to seek targets for our bullets, not to serve as such," retorted Sefton, somewhat angrily.

"Nay, I meant no offense, but I am not a stranger to these shores, as you are. The boats are ready, sir; fare you well."

Major Sefton touched his hat in grave salute, and was about to descend into the waiting boat where his officers were already seated, when a thought struck him and he stepped back to Captain Thornton's side.

" Your lady passenger " — he said, with somewhat heightened color, as the Captain smiled ; " do you desire me to bear a message to the fort, or have you already "—

" Yes," answered the captain, interrupting him suddenly, as the sun threw its first beams across the sparkling blue water, disclosing a small boat which had apparently just shoved off from the shore; "I sent Colonel Moncriffe word an hour after we had dropped anchor, and unless I mistake

yonder boat contains him, or some trusty escort for
his lovely daughter."

"Then will you say to Mistress Moncriffe" —

"Do not hinder Captain Thornton with even so
slight a thing as your message of farewell," said
a soft, slow voice behind them; "he is a most
busy officer and is surely relieved to find that his
task of looking after a troublesome maid is almost
over;" and Geraldine Moncriffe's radiant smile
deprived her words of their slight sting as she extended a slender hand to the somewhat embar-
rassed sailor. "What good fortune is mine to
come safe in port, with such near prospect of seeing my beloved and honored father!"

"And that fast approaching boat is fetching
him to you, madam; this, then, is our farewell,"
replied Major Sefton as the captain hurried off
to the ship's side.

"Nay, why say farewell in so tragic a tone? I
am but going to my father's plantation, a short
distance from Savannah, and the officers from the
fort will ever be welcomed by him. Surely Major
Sefton knows that the American loyalists serve
the king as well as those of His Majesty's subjects who have the good fortune to be born on
English soil."

"I can believe nothing but good of you and
yours," murmured the officer, pressing her hand as
he dropped his plumed hat, and hurried down the
side of the ship toward the waiting boat. Geraldine
Moncriffe drew her long cloak around her, and

leaned ever so lightly against the rail, shading her
eyes with her hand as she gazed anxiously in the
direction of the small boat which she had been
told was bringing Colonel Moncriffe to the vessel.

As the beams of the now risen sun struck the tall
masts of the Vigilant and fell aslant the girl's up-
raised face, there could be but one opinion as to
her singularly great beauty. It was not so much
the contour of her face and form, nor even the
finely cut features, but her coloring, which added
to her unusual and striking appearance, and gave
her an air of much distinction. Her skin was
extremely fair, and the tint of pink in her cheeks
was like the heart of a wild-rose, while her eye-
brows were very dark, though delicately penciled.
Her hair, from which her hood had fallen slightly
back, was a marvelous wreath of color,— a red-
golden, rather than a golden-red, so peculiar in
shade that once seen it impressed itself upon the
imagination from its striking contrast with her
eyes. For when Geraldine Moncriffe lifted her
long, dark lashes, there flashed upon you, instead
of the brown eyes one expected to see, the most
expressive pair of blue ones that ever adorned a
girl's face, — eyes at once frank, tender, bewitching, haughty, and proud, but never cold; and it
was this strange, crowning beauty which had made
her the toast of a brief London season as " the
Blue Bell of Scotland, — the fair Moncriffe."

Faster and faster came the little boat she was
watching toward the vessel, and as it rocked in the

swell caused by the departing troop boats, Geraldine saw the tall cloaked figure sitting in the stern raise his hand to shade his eyes as he eagerly surveyed the ship's side.

"I am here, father," she called, and the clear, soft voice carried well, for Colonel Moncriffe bared his head and waved his hand in reply, as he urged his oarsmen to greater speed, while Geraldine sped lightly along the deck, just in time to see her father greet Captain Thornton as he climbed the ship's companion-way; — the next minute she was clasped in his arms.

"And where is Margot?" asked the colonel, surveying his daughter with proud satisfaction as she stood blushing before him; "it was an unprecedented bit of good luck which enabled me to procure passage for you on this ship, and Lady Adair only obtained it through the very highest influence; but since this pestilent war we royalists must chance it as we may, and I rested tranquil in the assurance that you would be safe under charge of Margot, for nothing escapes her watchful eyes."

"Here she is," said Geraldine, turning toward the tall, gaunt figure who had quietly followed her down the deck and taken a position just behind them in time to hear the last remark.

"My grateful duty to you, Colonel Moncriffe; the night wad be dark and the day long that didna see auld Margot caring for her pretty bairn."

"Aye, Margot," and the colonel extended his hand to the fine-looking Scotchwoman who, with the plaid around her shoulders, seemed to bring with her a breath from the hills and moors of his boyhood, where Margot's mother had been his foster-mother as well. " My sister said I needed no better guardian than you, and from Geraldine's appearance the voyage has done her no harm."

" We have had favorable winds most of the way, and Captain Thornton thinks us good sailors. Are the boxes ready, Margot? I am impatient to be off, father, and long to see Glengarry again."

" We are to breakfast at the fort," said Colonel Moncriffe, " and the somewhat chilly air gives me a sharp appetite. This way, then ; " and he conducted them to the companion-way where Captain Thornton was waiting to make his farewell. With a light, sure foot Geraldine made her descent, and Margot clambered after, shutting her eyes tight and clinging to the sailor who assisted her on board the little boat with a grasp that made his fingers tingle with reminiscence for some minutes. Then the colonel, uttering courtly thanks, sprang down beside them, and the boat shoved off, while Geraldine waved adieu to the good ship which had brought her safe to port.

Fort Wayne looked grim and battered in the morning sunshine as the boat sped on its return trip to shore. On the land side were gangs of negroes busily at work upon the fortifications which had suffered so severely at the time of the siege, some months before. So determined and obstinate had been the attack of the Americans,

that the bitterest feeling still existed among the
conquerors, and many families of birth and position
had been compelled to flee from the city in various
directions by the victorious British. Indeed, so
greatly incensed were the invaders that they
offered a reward of two guineas for every citizen
known to adhere to the cause of the Whigs, and
the country-folk and negroes bringing produce and
vegetables into Savannah after the surrender were
forbidden to sell except to those who had taken
the oath of allegiance to King George. Had it
not been that there were many faithful souls who
continued to supply them with food, even under
these stringent and cruel conditions, the little
band of patriots who still dared occupy their
homes would have suffered starvation, and perhaps
death.

To Geraldine, coming across the bay, there had
been few more charming events than her return
to the land of the palmetto. Her three years' absence had but increased her love for her native
land, where she grieved sorely that rebellion had
broken forth against the authority which she had
been taught to reverence and honor. Even in
London, when her aunts, Lady Adair and Lady
Moncriffe, had presented her at court and in society, her cheeks would flush and her eyes fire at
the sneers and abuse leveled upon the colonists;
the haughty pride which her father had always
fostered forbade her to disown her country, and
deep down in her heart, below loyalty to king and

crown, there smouldered hot resentment which might some day astonish her by its awakening.

"Father," she asked, after Colonel Moncriffe had pointed out the havoc made by shot and shell in the fort, "your letters have left much untold. What of my friends — the girls I loved and played with? the Daytons, the Houstons, and above all my dear, lovely Rose Telfair? For some cause unknown to me, it is almost a year since I have heard from Rose, and " —

"Say no more," said her father sternly, " for that there is ample reason. The Houstons are here ; the Daytons gone to New York ; but the Telfairs are the most pestilent of Whigs and rebels, and since the absence of his father, young Telfair, it is said, has joined Marion's men in the partisan warfare which is a disgrace to the South."

"Marion's men ? Nay, father, I am perfectly ignorant of whom you speak.   Who is Marion?"

"The 'Swamp Fox,' [1] — the man who conducts a band of cut-throats and thieves in irregular raids upon our soldiers at most unexpected points ; who is hated, and I must admit feared, more than any other in the rebel ranks.   'T is a disagreeable and unprofitable subject, my daughter.   Let us dismiss it," — as the boat's keel grated on the land below the fort, — " and with all my heart I bid you welcome home ! "

So busily employed was the colonel in assisting Geraldine ashore, that he did not see a bit of

---

[1] The name given Colonel Marion by the British.

quick pantomime which took place on the boat behind him. As Margot rose to her feet the oars-
man nearest her drew in his oar, and under pre-
tense of guiding her steps, laid his hand upon her
arm. Margot's keen blue eyes looked swiftly into
his; and under her plaid he passed a bit of gray
moss, and as her fingers closed on it he said in her
ear, " To-morrow night, at ten ! "   .

CHAPTER II

IN MUSGROVE SWAMP

" HAVE care, sir; why do you jostle me so rudely? I think the street wide enough for both you and me."

" I crave your pardon, sir ; I am sorely troubled with my eyesight and am usually given right of way."

The street was long and narrow, and led westerly through the burned and deserted section of Savannah. Beyond the winds were sighing softly above Musgrove Swamp, for the tide was running in, and with no moon to light the way, all that the eye could see in the starlight was an expanse of water and what might be quicksand to any but one who knew the locality well.

The first speaker wore a British uniform, but his manner was so unusually civil that the other eyed him somewhat keenly, notwithstanding his excuse of blindness. The officer had taken a hasty step in the direction of the city, when a sudden reflection made him pause.

" As I have lost my way once I may do so again ; can you inform me how I may reach the fort?"

" Yes," answered a slow, drawling voice, as a slouching figure revealed itself on the left of the first speaker ; " ef yo' keep 'long to the right till yo' come to a baker's shop, an' just beyond that a blacksmith's, go down to the left an' yo' 'll get there."

" I am obliged to you ; I arrived by ship to-day from England and am not yet familiar with your city ; " and the officer was presently lost to sight in the darkness.

" He will hardly reach the fort before morning if he follows your trustworthy directions," said the other to his rustic companion as they resumed their way, picking their steps carefully in order to avoid the débris of the ruins around them.

" But he will be well on the way to Thunderbolt unless some equally veracious wayfarer come to his rescue. 'T is but seldom one has opportunity to be-devil a Britisher in civil fashion. He seemed a trifle more courteous than usual."

" Aye ; that 's because he has but just landed and has no experience with ' Yankee curs.' 'Gad, it 's dark," stumbling over an obstruction lying directly across the foot-path they followed. " The place of meeting should not be very far distant now, — hark ! "

A low note of the whip-poor-will sounded softly to the left, and turning suddenly in its direction, the pair found themselves confronted by a tall form wrapped in an Indian blanket.

" *Ossaba !* " said the newcomer softly. The

rustic pushed his companion aside quickly as he returned the countersign.

" *Laceola;* where are the others? "

The Indian made no response, but walked swiftly and steadily on, as he motioned them to follow, and presently the little party turned past a tall chimney which had apparently formed part of a stone house. To this there still remained a sort of vault, or cellar, and at the entrance stood a short, stout man, dressed in homespun.

" He is here," said the Indian, drawing back, and the whole party crawled through the narrow opening in silence. Inside was a good-sized room, its walls somewhat damp, which showed that the tides that flooded Musgrove Swamp had sometimes penetrated the outskirts of the city itself. A pine-knot torch was stuck between two projecting stones, and its flickering light disclosed a group of men, who were talking earnestly in low tones. They started apart, at the sound of approaching footsteps, and darting forward one of them struck the tall stranger on the shoulder.

" Welcome, welcome, McKay," he exclaimed. " We have expected you since last week, when one of the Legion brought your message."

" I was detained on the way and lay over at Snow Island."

" Then you bring news from Colonel Marion; how fares he, and the cause? "

" That question were better answered by another," returned Captain McKay, stepping aside as his rustic companion dropped his cloak and stood erect before them.

"The 'Swamp Fox' himself!" cried the eager speaker, as he flung his arm over Marion's shoulder, while every man pressed forward to wring the hand of the famous partisan leader, the "Washington of the South."

The little gathering of ten counted some of the best known and most loyal of the patriots of Georgia; tall, muscular men, with stern, set faces, and of military carriage. Among them the small, wiry form of Marion seemed almost insignificant, until you gazed into his eyes, which gleamed beneath the heavy brows with the fire, acuteness, and undying determination which was the keynote of his character. As he grasped the hand of each man in turn, the courtesy of his manner and the genial smile of friendly recognition gave evidence of the kindly heart and generous qualities which made men willing to follow wherever he led, and, if need be, to die with him in defense of their liberty.

"Gentlemen," said Marion, "the time presses, for I am somewhat late in reaching you. You see our situation; you have heard of the battle — aye, more than battle — the massacre of Waxham Creek, when Colonel Tarleton put all who surrendered to the sword, and you know what you yourselves have suffered in Savannah and the surrounding country. I have sworn an oath to Almighty God that while the heart of Marion

beats my eye will not relax its vigilance, nor my
arm its effort, to defend the cause of my country
and rid it of its oppressors. Gentlemen, you are
with me,"— for a low murmur of assent filled the
narrow room. "You were to have prepared for
Captain McKay a memorandum of names and
resources of the patriots here in Savannah, so that
when my raids are made I may know who are for
and who against us. Let me have the papers, and
then I must away, to a rendezvous on the farther
outskirts of Musgrove Swamp, where important
news awaits me."

Silently the little band of patriots gave into
Marion's hand the slips of paper so pregnant with
danger to themselves if discovered by the enemy,
and with a gesture of farewell to their gallant
leader, they filed quietly, one by one, out of the
vault, and scattered in various directions. By the
flickering light of the pine-knot torch Marion's eye
ran swiftly through the papers; then he placed
them carefully in a wallet, and concealed them on
his person.

"Extinguish the torch, Ossaba," he said briefly,
to the Indian who stood waiting beside the entrance, "and then lead on to the boat. McKay,
go first," and with careful steps the three men
went out into the night.

The wind had risen somewhat, and the sound of
the small waves of the incoming tide was plainly
perceptible as, after walking some half a mile
farther, they came to the shore. The Indian

waded out a few feet, and groping under the gray moss which hung from the trees on the edge of the bank drew out a canoe into which the two officers stepped easily. As Colonel Marion seated himself his hand came in contact with something soft, like a mantle, and he stooped to examine it.

" Woman went first," muttered the Indian, as he plied the paddle with due caution; "left blanket behind."

" Then the messenger has gone to the hut," whispered McKay. Marion nodded, and the boat glided on its way in silence through the swampy waters which extended for some distance west of the city and really formed one of the natural defenses of Savannah.

Ossaba, with the unerring instinct of his race, seemed able to avoid swags or too thick grasses which might have impeded their progress; indeed, there undoubtedly was a water-trail which he knew well, for after steadily paddling some twenty minutes, he shot the little boat swiftly into a small bend of the shore, which in clearer water might have been styled a cove, and standing up, separated the gray moss which swept down almost to the heads of the seated men, as the bottom grated softly in the sand.

" Wait with the boat, Ossaba," said Marion, and the Indian sank back on the seat. A few yards away on the right, far enough to be beyond the inroads of the tide-water, was a low, rude hut, so carefully concealed among the underbrush and moss as to be unperceived by any but those who knew of its existence. To this hut, Marion guided Captain McKay, and pausing at the low door which was roughly but securely barred, he whispered the countersign — " *Laceola*." A glimmer of light followed the whisper, and in another second the bar was undone, and on the threshold stood a tall, manly figure dressed in what resembled a hunting-shirt of dark green. Brown leggings encased his shapely legs, and a pair of pistols were stuck in his belt, while a broad, low hat was pushed carelessly on the back of a crop of wavy chestnut hair.

" Safe, thank God ! " he cried, wringing Marion's hand as he entered. " I 've had fifty minds in the last hour to go in search of you, fearing your capture in yonder unhappy city."

" You had been foolish to try it," said Marion dryly, but with an indulgent smile, as he gazed up into Roy Telfair's handsome face, " and beside the messenger "—

" She is here," interrupted the other, " and it 's well you finally arrived, colonel, for not a penny of the much needed treasure would Margot intrust to my hands. Faith, I think she suspects me of turning loyalist in her absence."

" I wad ken ye by the joke ye are fain to crack," was the quick retort, as Margot's gaunt figure rose from a cricket by the one window (or the opening that passed for such) that the hut boasted of. " My duty to you, sir — that is, if it be really

Colonel Marion, an' not another of Maister Roy's jokes."

"I am he, good woman." Margot curtsied respectfully. "But how's this, Telfair? I looked for a messenger in kilts, not skirts."

A slight flush rose to Margot's cheek. "I wadna contradict your Excellency; mayhap the kilt wad suit the emergency better, but the laird took what he had nearest at hand, and a Scotch tongue does na tattle whether it be hung in a mon's head or a woman's."

"She has you there, colonel," said McKay, laughing, while Marion hastened to soothe Margot's feelings by remarking that he, too, had been but joking.

"I'm thinking it's the way o' the land," said Margot with fine satire. "Here is the packet, sir, and right glad am I to surrender my charge, for many a sleepless night it's caused me since it was put in my keeping," and with another courtesy she returned to the window, where she stood respectfully out of earshot, as Marion broke the seal, and opened the packet.

"Our friends of the cause in Scotland have done nobly; here are five hundred pounds in notes, gentlemen. Most of this goes to aid our suffering soldiers; the rest for arms and ammunition. Stay, here is a letter from McAlpine," and he ran his eye hastily over the paper. "Listen; this is a clever way of forwarding aid to us rebels, is it not? McAlpine says: 'I lost my chance on the sloop,

as she carried no passengers, but this woman (one
of my clan) goes over as passenger in His Majesty's ship Vigilant, being nurse and escort to the
daughter of Colonel Moncriffe — '"

" Moncriffe!" ejaculated McKay, "this is indeed a merry stratagem."—

"'And,'" continued Marion, smiling, "'knowing you are sore bestead in the provinces, I send
it, being assured that no search will be made of
the belongings of so good a loyalist as Miss Moncriffe.'"

"This is after your own heart," laughed McKay,
"setting a loyalist to guard money for such
'pestilent rebels' as we! You seem to know the
old woman, Telfair; who and what is she?"

"Margot McAlpine was half-sister to the Scotchwoman who nursed my sister Rose and me," said
Roy coldly. "My father's plantation adjoined
that of the Moncriffes', and since we were babies
we have been friends until the colonies rose
against British rule. Colonel Moncriffe remained
loyal to the crown, and sent his only child three
years ago to finish her education in England and
Scotland. It is scarcely to be wondered that
Mistress Moncriffe remains true to the principles
of her family."

Colonel Marion looked up from the paper he
had been studying; he detected the under-tone of
irritation in Roy's voice, and with the wonderful
tact for which he was noted interposed at once.

"We have still some miles to travel, and the

night is safest for our undertaking, McKay. You, Telfair, had best wait here for another twenty-four hours, as I think you told me you had some family matters to attend to. But, I beseech you, see to those with due care of your own safety, and join your command as soon as may be, as I have other work for you. Ossaba remains with the skiff; do you desire him to take the Scotch woman back to Savannah?"

"It is the way she came, and she would be missed by daylight. I will escort her to the edge of the swamp. Farewell, Colonel; I will finish my private affair and join at once. McKay, your most obedient. Come, Margot, we will to the boat."

Margot drew her plaid around her shoulders, and the young man took her hand to lead her through the darkness as they left the hut. He had nearly reached the shore before he spoke.

"Margot, stop a moment. You have told me no word as yet of Geraldine. Is she lovelier than ever? or is she changed and grown into the manners and ways of the court since she left these humbler colonies?"

"She was always a bonny bairn," said Margot, cautiously, "and she has a deft way wi' her noo! Changed, aye; if you ca' changed to be mair beautiful and mair haughty than iver. I dinna ken quite what's in her mind; she'd scoff and flout the gay gallants in Edinburgh an' London till they were fit to tear their hair wi' vexation. But

she has the same soft, winsome smile, and her
sweet, sweet voice wad wile a bird off yonder bush.
I dinna say that she's coquette, but to my mind
there's mony shades of that same complaint.
D'ye ken what they call her over there in London? the 'Blue Bell o' Scotland;' and I heard
the officers at Leddy Moncriffe's dinner toasting
her by that bonny name. She's different since
ye saw her, Maister Roy, but somehow her auld
nurse thinks she's the same at the bottom of her
heart, and she'll aye be leal and true to her ain
people."

Roy's hand closed warmly over Margot's as he
led her on to the boat. "Thank you," he said
simply; "I dare not send a message, for the giving
it would reveal that you have seen me. But, Margot, I am coming into the city to see my mother
and Rose, and I may contrive to be somewhere
near Geraldine. I may not reveal myself, but I
own I'd like a glimpse of my old playmate. Here
is the boat, Ossaba; return to the city with the
pale-face woman, but moor the boat safely again
for me on your return. Farewell, Margot," and
he bent over and kissed the faithful Scotch woman
as he shoved the boat from shore, then hurried
back to the hut, whistling softly under his breath
as he went. But after he passed the spot where
he had paused in the path to question Margot, the
long branches of an overhanging tree were separated by a slim, dark hand; first a girl's face
looked carefully out between the gray moss cur-

A GIRL'S FACE LOOKED CAREFULLY OUT

tain which clung to the branches, then slowly a graceful figure stepped forth, as she peered into the darkness with her hand shading her eyes.

"He talked of the pale-faced maiden to her," she murmured to herself; "it is the same long name he whispered in his sleep under the trees yesterday. Laceola will remember; Laceola can wait."

CHAPTER III

AN OFFICER OF THE KING

It was about seven o'clock in the morning, and the thrifty little village of Ebenezer, which lay some twenty-five miles distant from Savannah, looked awake and in motion. Early in the history of Georgia it had been settled by the Saltzburgers, a shrewd, grave colony of men and women, who sought there freedom of religious opinion, and who, when the war for Independence dawned, promptly declared themselves upon the side of the patriots, with but few exceptions. So determined were the Germans in giving aid to the Continentals that the colony became a source of menace to the British, who, a year or more before, took forcible possession of it, and Colonel Maitland, the officer in command, had left and still maintained a garrison there.

A comely-looking woman of middle age came slowly down the street which led through the village, accompanying a stout boy of twelve who led a horse by the halter. It was a rather unkempt nag, and somewhat thin, and its gait was rendered uneven by its lack of a shoe, which gave it a queer amble enough.

"Franz," said the woman, speaking in German, but with a pleasant voice, "did thy father say at what hour to-morrow he would meet thee at the turn of the road?"

"No, mother," answered the lad in the same tongue, "but I am to fetch the cart also."

"Then there be others coming," said the woman, half to herself, as they turned aside, and walking a few steps farther stopped before a blacksmith's shop, where the fire had not yet been lit in the smithy. "Give me the halter, Franz; I'll hold the beast while thou go call Wilhelm," and she sat down on a convenient tree stump as Franz opened a gate and ran up the path which led to the blacksmith's house.

Presently a stout, burly figure was seen, accompanied by another, a half-grown fellow, who carried a bellows and a bit of burning wood on a shovel, which would serve to light the fire. Franz ran nimbly ahead, and took the halter from his mother as she rose from her seat.

"A fine spring morning, Frau Hartzel. I am sorry to have kept you waiting, but the house-mother has gone to the pasture for the cow, and I was giving little Gottlieb his bread and butter. Why, the horse has been unlucky to lose another shoe," examining that animal, as his apprentice and Franz set eagerly to work blowing the fire; "it was only last night that" —

"Aye," interrupted the woman hastily, "but

the beast has been on a long journey since, where
the way was rough, and I only wonder it did not
lame him far worse. And he's needed for more
work to-morrow, so I brought him up early lest
others might observe."

"The redcoats have spared him so far; you
are more in luck than some of us."

"That's because he's not much for looks,"
was the shrewd answer, as Frau Hartzel followed
the blacksmith inside the smithy; "there are few
can outstrip the old beast when Hans has need of
speed. Shoe him as fast as you are able, Wilhelm; I'd not like to be stopped and questioned
by the British patrol on our way back."

"Then you did not pass the church on the
way?" The blacksmith hurried to his anvil, then
came back and took up the horse's fore foot and
inspected it carefully.

"What's amiss?"

"Naught," returned the man, but with a twinkle
of his blue eye, as he passed his hand over the
fetlock; "that shoe is no mate to any in Ebenezer, though I can make good guess whence it
came."

"Tell me," whispered the woman, getting closer
that the two lads might not hear the conversation.

"The farrier that nailed that shoe is many a
mile from here, guten Frau. It bears the private
mark of the Swamp Fox; behold!" and raising
the hoof again cautiously he placed his finger on a
rudely scrawled Indian arrowhead. "Hans will

tell you that is why the Swamp Fox's men never miss the trail of their own rangers.[1]   But let it not pass your tongue; the secret is of great value so long as the British are in ignorance of it.   Here, Franz, hold the halter; I'll have the shoe on quickly."

Frau Hartzel mused for a moment, and was about to return to her seat on the tree stump outside when a sound of horses' feet made her turn her head.   Coming up the street were two men, mounted, followed by four others.   The two in advance were evidently officers, both young men; one wore the uniform of the Georgia loyalists (a body of Tory troopers, made up partly of New Yorkers and South Carolinians as well), and the other, a strikingly handsome fellow, was dressed in full panoply of scarlet and gold lace, which the trappings proclaimed to be that of a lieutenant-colonel in His Britannic Majesty's service.   The officer's carriage was military in the highest degree; his figure was tall and erect, and he sat his horse with ease and grace.   Under his heavy brows a pair of fine dark eyes flashed, which were both keen and relentless; his nose was slightly aquiline, but not too prominent, and gave strength to the face; his complexion clear and of olive tint, while his mouth and chin were of the most determined character, — a face of infinite possibilities and contradictions, proud, inscrutable, and fascinating; but to a close observer the smile which at

[1] See Lee's Memoirs.

that moment lit his countenance, as he turned his head toward his companion, was full of satire, and there was a cruel gleam in the handsome eyes which belied his calm, tranquil voice. Such, at the age of twenty-six, was Colonel Banastre Tarleton, a man feared by many, hated by more, and known by none.

The little party were entering the village from the north, and as they drew near the blacksmith's shop one of the four troopers, who apparently formed the escort, rode forward and addressed Tarleton.

"If the colonel pleases," he said, saluting respectfully, "the hind shoes of my horse are loose, and I fear he will lose them before we reach Savannah. Shall I have them tightened by this man?"

Tarleton turned quickly and drew in his rein. He was always solicitous as to his men's equipment, and especially as regarded the horses. "Hallo, fellow," he said imperiously, addressing Wilhelm, "quit fumbling with that sorry-looking beast and attend to my horse here. His shoes want fastening securely, as we have a journey to finish before nightfall, and here's sixpence for your pains," and tossing the coin carelessly in the direction of the smith Tarleton rode down the street to the brick church, once the pride of the people of Ebenezer, but now occupied as hospital and stable by the British.

Wilhelm went leisurely on driving the nail on

which he was working, as the trooper flung himself from the saddle. Frau Hartzel drew away into the corner of the smithy, motioning Franz to take the halter she dropped, which he did with alacrity.

"There," ejaculated the blacksmith, resting his hammer as he lowered the horse's foot and stood upright. "'T is a job well done. Nay, lad," as Franz produced a coin from his pocket, "thy father and I are old neighbors — I keep no account with such. Give it to your mother; I'll come and share thy dish of sauerkraut, Franz, to-morrow night."

"You have a seeming lack of regard for money," said the trooper, as he loosened his coat and leaned up against the side of the smithy. "Yonder is the sixpence the colonel flung ye; for my part I do not treat a likeness of His Majesty so lightly. Why did you not stoop to pick it up? We hear that you people of Ebenezer are a very pestilent lot, but you are a fool to let your politics have the ordering of your pockets."

"Belike," returned the smith dryly.

"It's well the colonel did not see you scorn his gift."

"Gift, man? 't is my honest earning."

"Then why not lift it off the ground?" pursued his tormentor.

"No one is likely to steal it; we are honest folk here in Ebenezer."

"You handle the hammer well; 't is a pity so

stout a fellow as you should stop here in these troublous times. Why — as you will not accept His Majesty's sixpence — why not take the king's shilling and join our company? It's a life full of adventure, and I'm in search of recruits since this last affair at Waxham Creek."

"Where be that? Is it a battle, and did you redcoats win it?"

"A battle! Aye, a slaughter, for the place ran red with rebel blood before Tarleton sheathed his sword. The rebels cried out for 'quarter, quarter,' and the legion stabbed and shot them as they lay wounded along the banks of the creek till darkness came down" —

"Ah!" Frau Hartzel could not restrain a faint cry of horror.

"Go home, Frau," said Wilhelm shortly, as the shuddering woman, followed by the boys with the horse, passed out of the smithy. "What are ye made of, man, that ye stand and tell bragging tales of such hellish work? Quarter asked, and none given! Such news as that will send every Saltzburger in Ebenezer who remains true to king and crown into the ranks of the patriots. Out of my smithy, and take thy nag with thee; he is too good an animal to carry such a beast as thou;" and the burly German rushed upon the trooper with such sudden force that he bore him to the ground before he had opportunity to draw a weapon.

"Enough, enough," shouted the trooper, as

Wilhelm raised his great fist for another strike;
" this is more than I had cause to expect, much
as I desired to prove you. Have you forgotten
a night last March on the edge of Musgrove
Swamp " —

"Thou — thou?   I begin to see thy face is
known to me.   But where is thy beard? and what
brings thee here in the train of yonder monster of
cruelty?"

"Hush!" The trooper rose, shook the dust off
his coat, and glanced cautiously up and down the
road. "By command of the Swamp Fox two
months ago I left Snow Island, and turned up at
Charleston with a clever tale of starvation and
wrongs at the hands of the patriots. Colonel
Tarleton was busy recruiting for his legion, and
I enlisted with him.   I have been on several raids
without exciting suspicion, but this horrible affair
at Waxham has tried me sorely.   God! how those
men were slaughtered!   Had I not been detailed
as guard with some others to protect the baggage
of the officers in the rear I would have deserted;
aye, had I even seen the butchers at their work
I must have struck a blow for my countrymen.
I did not know till too late to succor, and even
after the fight, received from a fugitive whom I
helped escape, orders of grave importance from
Colonel Marion.   Hark ye," — he put his mouth
almost at the smith's ear and whispered softly, —
" I am a special spy on Tarleton, and have managed to ingratiate myself with him.   We are on

the road to Savannah, where no doubt he goes to
plot further deviltries, and I must establish a trail
here to convey information I may send.   I remem-
bered you the instant I saw we were to pass Ebenezer, and I contrived to loosen those shoes an
hour ago."

"Good ; what can I do for thee ? "   The trooper
passed around to the other side of his horse, who
stood waiting with head patiently bowed.   From
beneath the saddle he drew forth a scrap of chamois
skin on which were scrawled some rude characters
which looked like Indian pictures.

"This must reach the Swamp Fox in safety ;
can you take it, or have you others by whom to
send it ? "

"Hans Hartzel ; he comes to-morrow.   That
was his wife here, and his horse, and I know by
unfailing signs that he has lately been in close
communication with the patriots."

"Take it then," — the sound of a bugle came
floating up on the morning air ; " I have been
full long over that loose shoe."   He sprang into
the saddle, but the smith's hand detained him.

"Your name — in case I have to use it."

"Oh, aye ; Burt, Norman Burt.   That 's my
name now ; perhaps I may confess to another
some day," and the trooper trotted off in the direction of the church, as the smith went back to
his anvil.

The Lutheran church of Ebenezer was a square,
low structure, and had been the principal building

of the place, but now, divided as it was into
part hospital, part stable, its desecration and filth
were a source of burning wrath to the inhabitants.
Just beyond the church was a wooden house
painted white, formerly the parsonage, but the
minister had been driven away and it was used as
headquarters of the garrison by the British.   Inside the low portal could be seen a table spread
with food, and seated at it with several others were
Colonel Tarleton and Captain Israel Halleck, of
the Georgia loyalists, who at that time formed one
of Tarleton's military family, and was probably
his only intimate friend.

The officers stationed at the post were evidently
delighted to entertain Colonel Tarleton, for the
room rang with laughter and jest, and the breakfast was prolonged half an hour to permit the
horses to be baited.   At the end of that time,
Tarleton drew back his chair, and buckling on
his sword walked out on the low veranda which
ran around two sides of the house.

"I have ordered an Indian scout to give you
the trail for some eight miles of the way, colonel;
after that the road lies straight ahead to Savannah," said Captain Conway, the officer in command.   "Are either of your fellows familiar with
these parts?"

"The trooper holding my horses is our guide;
he is a Georgian and has keen eyes for a trail.
Can I do anything for you, Conway, in the
city?"

"Nothing except to beseech the commandant to relieve me," laughed Conway; "it's so devilish dull at this post of psalm-singing, sauerkraut Germans that I'd exchange to field duty with most cheerful alacrity. Farewell, Tarleton; fortune favor your mission whatever it be."

Colonel Tarleton trotted briskly off, with Halleck following, but after going a half mile he drew rein and waited for his friend to ride beside him.

"Conway little knows," he said with a laugh, "what my so-called mission may be. Of course, the military part of it we have discussed, but that which relates to love, not war, is something I have reserved for your private ear."

"I suspected as much," said the other dryly; "there is usually the swish of a gown to be heard in your pathway."

"What would the world be without women for our lighter hours, man? I've had battles enough for a while, and can afford to dally a little with mine own affair. You may recollect the packet which came express to me a month ago before we left Charleston? Well, 'tis of that I wish to tell you.

"You have, I think, already met Colonel Moncriffe of our army. He was born in Scotland, but took an American wife and is one of the staunchest adherents to the crown in the provinces. My father and he were bosom friends long before their respective marriages, and pledged each other that the friendship should be continued by a union between their children (should the Lord be pleased to vouchsafe them olive-branches) in the future. Behold in me the party of the first part; the fair Geraldine Moncriffe the party of the second."

"You do surprise me, Tarleton. Is is possible that you, the fickle, the changeful, the fastidious Tarleton, are about to concentrate your affections upon one fair damsel, leaving numberless victims to mourn your capture!"

"Mock me as you will," said Tarleton, with a satirical smile; "you have not yet heard the story. A year ago, I had intimation from my father that the Moncriffe, in addition to her charms of face and form, will be a very great heiress, for this part of the world, and a goodly one even in old England. Whether the colonel has found a gold mine in this pestilent country or no, the golden casket, with its accompanying jewel, lies waiting for me; and perhaps I am rendered more keen in pursuit of my fair quarry by a miniature which the lady's father was good enough to forward me in the packet which reached me at Charleston. What think you of that face, Halleck? Be she but one half as beautiful she will serve to make profound love to — for a month." As he spoke, Tarleton drew from an inner pocket a small case which he handed to his friend, and an exclamation of surprise and admiration burst from Halleck's lips as he opened it and there flashed upon his gaze Geraldine Moncriffe's exquisite

beauty, painted by one of the great artists of the
day.

"You are right! What glorious eyes, what
superb coloring! I wonder if 't is true to life."

"It can hardly be less, for my father writes that
she has been the toast in town this season, and by
a fanciful title, the 'Blue Bell of Scotland.'"

"She 's divine! Here, take back your portrait,
or I shall be tempted to enter the lists myself."

"Against me? Pray do; jealousy and strife
will give the needed flavor to my suit; my only
fear is that the conquest — backed by her father
— may be too easy a one."

"Fie, Tarleton; I begin to believe that the
New York dames and damsels have turned your
brain with their attentions, only I do remind me
that Mistress Betty Wolcott turned a deaf ear" —

"Hold, sir, you go too far," interrupted Tarleton haughtily, as he thrust the case inside his
coat. Then, after a moment, he added in a softer
tone, "The shoe pinches not so much as you think,
Halleck, but I own I have not yet forgotten that
pretty rebel. I wonder if the fair Moncriffe possesses the same charm; one cannot have everything, and fascination combined with beauty
grows not on every bush."

Their horses going at a fairly good speed, it did
not take long to reach the end of the trail for
which the little party had been offered the services of Captain Conway's Indian scout, and after
his departure they resumed their way, which led

partly through woodland, from which glimpses might be occasionally had of the river winding on its way south. When the sun overhead proclaimed noon, Tarleton ordered a halt, and under shade of a great tree and its curtain of gray moss they rested the horses and took a drink from the flasks which the officers carried, the men having some provisions in the saddlebags. But Tarleton, impatient to be off, cut short their meal (such as it was), and mounting, desired the trooper Burt to ride ahead, as he knew the trail.

" 'T is ticklish business," muttered Burt to himself, as he tightened his stirrup and trotted on. " We may strike the Rangers at any moment, and then — Gad, I 'd not like to bite the dust of Georgia soil by a shot from my old comrades. But I 'd cheerfully lose a leg or arm to get yonder fiend into Marion's hands. Those bushes at the right have been recently bent ; the twigs are wilting in the sun," and then, as the thought flashed through his brain, he saw, peering at him in the thicket, a pair of glittering eyes.

Involuntarily, Burt's hand sought his pistol ; but before he could draw it from his belt, the bushes parted, and the slender, graceful figure of an Indian girl glided out on the path. Tall and well formed, her dark flowing hair was bound with a strip of scarlet cloth, fastened by an eagle's feather ; her blanket was slung around her shoulders with more than ordinary care, and on her feet were beautifully embroidered moccasins. On each shapely, bronzed arm she wore an armlet of roughly beaten silver, and around her neck a silver chain, from which hung the totem (the emblem of her tribe), a coiled rattlesnake, with its head reared as if to strike.

"Halt!" cried Tarleton, spurring forward, as his eye caught the strangely picturesque figure, but before he reached the spot Burt's quick perception had taken every detail of the girl's appearance, and under his breath he said softly, "Laceola!"

A slight quiver of the dainty nostrils was the only sign that betrayed her knowledge of the word; she stood motionless as Tarleton accosted her.

"Who are you, and from whence do you come?"

"I am Laceola, the sister of Ossaba."

"Where are you going, and why do you walk alone in the forest?"

"Laceola walks where she will," said the girl proudly; "the palefaces are kind to her. She goes to Yamacraw, where now is a settlement they call Savannah."

Tarleton hesitated a moment, and Burt took the opportunity to say in a low tone, "She is a Creek, and the colonel knows that tribe have been employed by the Tories in this war."

"Faith, Halleck," said Tarleton, with a laugh, "she has the air of a princess — this American savage. Come nearer, girl," and, as Laceola stepped fearlessly to his side, he stooped suddenly in his saddle and kissed her on the lips.

There was a flash and gleam of steel as a long knife shot into the air, and but for the swerving aside of his frightened horse, Tarleton's career had ended then and there. The knife grazed the horse's ear and buried itself in the green sward beyond, while the girl, panting for breath, stood with her small hands clenched, the embodiment of concentrated rage.

"Laceola has seen many pale-faced men — she has walked these forests alone both day and night; no Inglese, no Yankee, has harmed her. Redcoat, you are a villain; pah!" — and she drew her hand across her lips with a gesture of scorn and loathing, — "you are a coward!"

A red flush mounted to Tarleton's forehead, as he half drew his pistol, then dropped his hand, with a sneering laugh.

"'T is only a wildcat, after all. Burt, tie the girl's hands and mount her before you on the saddle; I 'll carry a prisoner with me into Savannah."

Halleck opened his lips to speak, then thought better of it, and in silence Burt dismounted, secured Laceola's hands, and, with the aid of the other troopers, placed her on his horse. But just as he was about to spring up behind her, the girl bent her head; swift as lightning she seized the reins, which lay loosely on the horse's neck, in her teeth, and, striking the animal a blow with her feet, in one second she was off, tearing like mad up the road, where a sudden bend hid her from

view almost before the men had time to grasp the
fact that their prisoner had escaped.

"To horse!" cried Tarleton; but the troopers
had barely sprung into their saddles before he
checked them. "Pursuit is useless; the jade will
have joined some lurking Indian by this, and I do
not care to be shot from ambush. Halleck, I was
a fool to try issue with a Creek; we have had
trouble enough with that nation."

"Aye," said Halleck dryly, "better let women
alone — if you can."

Tarleton laughed again; his good humor had
apparently returned, but the gleam in his eye
boded no good to Laceola even while he jested.

"'T was a clever escape, by Gad! the princess
has a ready wit. But you 'll have to ride double,
my man," to Burt, "or else foot it into Savannah."

Burt saluted, and went toward the other troopers,
but as he again put foot in the stirrup, a distant
neigh was heard, and as the party turned in its
direction, to their amazement they beheld the
missing horse, riderless, trotting rapidly back to
join its companions.

"By ——" Burt ripped out an oath. "Beg
pardon, colonel, but of all adventures" — and he
gazed blankly at the officers.

Halleck burst into a hearty laugh. "You must
e'en make the best of it, Tarleton; the wench
was honest enough to return your property, but
none will ever believe the tale of how an Indian
girl flouted the gay and gallant Tarleton," and

spurring their horses both friends galloped down the road.

But Burt, riding more slowly in their train, said to himself, "The Swamp Fox is not far away. I 'll wager the colonel has not heard the last of this pretty encounter."

CHAPTER IV

AT GLENMOIRA

THE mansion stood in the centre of a grove of live oaks and myrtle trees, and was an unusually fine specimen of the residence occupied by the rich planters of that day. It had been built by Madam Moncriffe's father, and added to in various ways at different times, until it presented a combination of quaintness, stability, and even elegance, being built chiefly of brick imported from England, as was then the custom, and in some part of wood after the fashion of the early days of the province. The plantation itself extended for miles, being part of the original letters-patent granted to Percival Heathcote, and then considered as belonging to the province of South Carolina. When the new province of Georgia was given to its trustees by King George the Second, the Heathcote of that day exchanged part of his land for that within the new grant, and, proceeding to plant rice in these most fertile swamps formed by the Savannah River, amassed what was for those days a handsome fortune, which, added to his hundred or more slaves, made him a power in that vicinity. Dying, he left an only daughter,

whom Colonel Moncriffe married, and it was a
noticeable fact that, although an officer in His
Majesty's service and a gallant soldier (as he had
proved himself during the siege of Savannah),
Colonel Moncriffe seemed to have a gift for
acquiring money outside his profession, and indulged in every extravagant fancy of the day.
Costly furniture, pictures, and china were always
coming from England for transportation to Glenmoira, and before the war broke out his elaborate
entertainments were the talk of the town. The
death of his wife, some four years previous,
had called a temporary halt in his gayeties, but
now that Geraldine had returned home with the
triumph of a London season hovering about her,
the Tory dames of Savannah gossiped behind
their fans as they met in the streets and at
each other's houses, and predicted that the re-
newal of hospitality would be speedy, and after
even more prodigal fashion than before.

The front of the house was most imposing, with
its tall white pillars, and square entrance flagged
with stone, whence the descent to the ground was
made by six broad, low steps. The wings stretched
to right and left, and were irregularly built, one
side being devoted to bedrooms, where bachelor
guests were bestowed, and the other running out
still further and used as servants' quarters; these
wings added much to the picturesque appearance
of the place, as they were completely covered by
vines which ran up even to the slanting roofs.

Near one of the large white pillars sat Geraldine on a low stool, two great baskets of roses beside her, and at her elbow a small table on which stood a huge blue china bowl which, with deft, busy fingers, she was engaged in filling with flowers. Her white gown (tied around the short waist with a broad blue ribbon) with its scanty skirt gave enchanting glimpses of the dainty feet beneath the petticoat, and became her well, while her red-gold hair, drawn up from the nape of her slender neck and piled in curling masses over her broad brow, seemed a fitting crown to her beauty.

" Hech ! but she 's bonnie," thought Margot, as she came out of the door, her hands filled with long, feathery sprays of green, " I wish Maister Roy could see her noo ! "

" Just in time, Margot ; oh, tell Jumbo to fetch me the tall blue jars from the mantel in my room. Nothing becomes deep red roses like them. Do you mind, Margot, "—falling into a little of the quaint Scotch phrase as she sometimes did when alone with her, — " do you mind how I used to greet for the red and white roses, and how my aunt scolded me because I said nothing could compare with our cherokee hedges of white ? Ah, Margot, 't is sweet to be in my own home once more ; to see the kindly black faces of the slaves, and hear them sing their plaintive songs at nightfall, and though I love the English nightingale's note, there 's a wild melody in the mocking bird which goes straight to the heart." Margot looked up quickly enough to see a tear that fell from her young mistress's eyes among the roses.

"You see, Margot," Geraldine went on, half talking, half thinking aloud, "London was grand and beautiful and stately — and I love to be stately and grand as well as most maids. But somehow last night when I rode down through the live-oaks with my father, and the wind blew a spray of gray moss across my face, and I heard a distant whip-poor-will, I thought of the days when I used to stand down yonder by the thicket, and how Rose Telfair and I made wreaths to deck my mother's grave, and Roy — oh, I wonder where Roy is now, Margot? My father says he has taken arms against the king. I could not have believed it of him. Think, think of being a rebel, Margot, and in arms against your country!"

"It depends mickle upon whilk country ye claim for your ain," quoth Margot, with a twinkle of fun in her shrewd bright eyes. "Some o' your forbears, I 'm thinking, puzzled over that question in the 'Forty-Five!'"

"Truly," and Geraldine laughed lightly at Margot's thrust. "But that was so different; we were fighting for a king, even then."

"An' the patriots are fighting for their lawful rights," said Margot stubbornly. "What I 'm thinking is that what 's sauce for the goose is like to be sauce for the gander in this war as in mony ithers."

"Margot, Margot, are you turning rebel? Oh,

for peace' sake do not let my father hear you. He has been giving me a long account to-day of the iniquitous doings of the partisans here, and truth to say my head is somewhat bewildered."

" Look yonder," interrupted Margot, suddenly waving her hand as the sound of a galloping horse was heard coming toward them. Geraldine's eye followed the gesture, and as she rose to her feet she saw a pretty picture. Over the thicket where grew the cherokee roses, some quarter of a mile from the house, came flying a handsome chestnut filly, her neck stretched high, her head well up as her heels cleared the top, and on her back a slender figure who, laughing and waving her hand in salute, galloped swiftly up to the door.

" Rose, Rose, my own dear Rose!" cried Geraldine, running down the steps just in time to catch the pretty creature who bounded from the saddle into her outstretched arms. " Rose!" — holding her at arm's length, and surveying every laughing feature — "it is really you, and just as *dear* and merry as when I left you three long years ago."

" And twenty times as naughty," returned the newcomer; " my father says I will never learn to be grown up and proper. But you — oh, Jerry, Jerry, to think you have seen the world, and even courtesied before the king — not that I love the king " — with a charming blush at tripping in her speech — " but the gay, beautiful London and the gallants there — though I do suppose I should

hate them violently if they dared sneer at us
' rebels.' "

" Rose, Rose, remember in whose house you
stand — and for the matter of that you know that
I am, as of old, a Tory."

Rose Telfair flashed a merry, wicked glance at
her friend as she ran lightly up the steps, and a
little black boy came running from the servants'
quarters to take the chestnut mare.

" A Tory? verily you have not that air, try as
you may. It's tiresome enough in the city where
the officers' dames turn their backs — and extremely
ugly, badly dressed backs they are to boot — and
endeavor not to see me, when if they but knew it
I would not stop and speak to them — no! not for
twenty pounds," and Rose ended more hotly than
she began.

" A truce to politics," said Geraldine gently.
" Here's Margot waiting for a word from you."
Margot courtesied, but the impulsive girl's arms
were thrown round her neck, and Rose kissed the
ruddy cheek with a hearty affection which brought
tears to the Scotchwoman's eyes.

" Ah, but you favor Maister Roy; the same
eyes wi' the laughing glint in them, the same waving chestnut hair, and will you never stop growing,
Mistress Rose," glancing up at the slender figure,
which was unusually tall for a woman; "mair by
token as ye overtop my young leddy."

" How do you know that I resemble Roy so
closely?" asked Rose with a mischievous smile,

which set Margot's cheeks tingling at her slip of
the tongue, but which Geraldine did not catch the
meaning of.

" Hoot, d' y' think I 've forgotten," said Margot,
recovering herself quickly. " Mony 's the time
Elspeth and I said ye might pass for twins, the
likeness was sae great between ye. Do ye need
mair flowers, Mistress Geraldine, or are these eno'
for the vases ? "

" Quite enough, Margot, and I 'll leave them to
you to finish. Rose and I are going to my own
room."

Inside the square hall rose a winding staircase
with solid mahogany balustrade, and the rooms
above opened on a gallery which ran around it.
Into one of these Geraldine guided Rose, and
pulling a high chair forward to the window seated
her guest, while she took refuge on a quaint settle
beside her.

" What a lovely room ! " said Rose ; " those curtains of pale yellow are most novel. And the bed
drapery is the same ; are these the last London
mode ? "

" My father ordered them last year, and I found
the room just as you see it when I arrived."

" And your gowns " — eagerly — " where are
your gowns, Geraldine ? I trust you come back
prepared to dazzle the eyes of the Tory dames in
Savannah, for we poor Whigs are fain to wear
last year's costumes, being too proud to ape those
of a foreign court."

"Gowns, aye; but let us not trouble with these just now, Rose. I—I have so much to say to you; have you patience to listen?"

"Surely; I meant no harm by my silly desire to see the wardrobe of a woman of fashion. What troubles you? or are you grown too staid to frolic with your old playfellow?"

"Never," said Geraldine, with quiet emphasis, "but I scarce feel in frolicsome mood to-day. What air would you think becoming to a maid who is bidden to receive a suitor who comes with her father's consent to ask her hand in marriage?"

"It would greatly depend on the suitor; who is he? what is he like? are you madly in love?" Rose poured out question after question, and Geraldine's laugh rang out blithely. It seemed impossible to be serious and sedate with Rose; evidently the gravity of the situation did not impress her.

"You have not changed a particle in these three years. How can I tell you what he is like when I have never yet set eyes on him?"

"Good lack! this is quite in royal fashion. And who may the suitor be?"

"Colonel Banastre Tarleton, of England, formerly aide to Lord Cornwallis; but my father tells me that he now commands a legion made up of Georgia and New York loyalists, and that he was most prominent at the taking of Charleston."

"Colonel Tarleton!" Rose ejaculated, then stopped short and bit her lip. "How comes it that you are plighted to him?"

" I am not plighted yet," responded Geraldine somewhat warmly.

" Oh, but you said "—

"That he comes here to-day, unless some ill fortune of war detain him.   You do misjudge me; am I the style of maiden who can be won before she is wooed?   My father is an old and bosom friend of Colonel Tarleton's father, and so — and so " —

" I see ; they have arranged the match between them.   Well?"

" I had not given you my confidence had I supposed you lacked interest in my fate," said Geraldine, with heightened color.

" Nay, nay," cried Rose, seizing her hand, " I did not mean to anger you.   Go on, tell me more ; you know how I love you.   It was my surprise that made me seem petulant.   Forgive it."

" I scarcely know what to say ; my father tells me the gentleman is young, handsome, brave, and rich.   Sometimes I think I am fortunate, then — I know not why — I loathe him."

" Is there " — Rose hesitated.   " Geraldine, is there perchance another? have you left your heart behind you in London?"

" No, no " — with burning cheeks.   " But dutiful daughter though I am and desire to be, I feel such strange reluctance to this project."

" Wait and see the gentleman," said Rose, with cool philosophy ; " did you say he was expected to-day ? "

"Yes, and my father has bidden a party from the fort to dine with us and to meet him, also several friends from the city. I heard Margot telling Jupiter to set the table and put out the new silver plate which came from England a month ago; did you not see me arranging the roses as you came in? Stay with me, Rose, and grace my first dinner with your charming presence."

"In my habit, and to meet all those redcoats? Truly, you forget that I am both Whig and rebel; I should be the skeleton at your feast."

"I have done nothing but talk of my own affairs and am self-reproached. 'T is my turn to question now as to the state of *your* affections," with mock gravity.

"I knew that would be your next question. No, the tender passion has not yet touched my heart. I am constant to my childish hero — my brother Roy."

"And Roy — what of him?" said Geraldine softly. "I did not ask because" —

"Because you have doubtless heard him called rebel and traitor," cried Rose; "do not fear to confess it. I have heard Colonel Moncriffe express his opinion to my father, and — in no measured terms — my father's reply."

"Alas, upon what times have I fallen to return to my country! Rose, Rose, do not let this war part you and me."

Rose sprang to her feet. "You have heard one view from your father; now hear mine. Because we will not take oath of allegiance to a king whose yoke we have thrown off and whose armies we have defeated, — aye, many times, — we are hounded like outlaws. Since Savannah has been taken by the British, since the siege. even the country-folk are forbidden to sell their produce to us, and rewards were offered by the British officers for the detection of every citizen who adhered to the Whig cause. Were not the Clark, the Dayton, and the McIntosh houses guarded and the women of the families confined within them, their only offense being that their fathers, sons, and brothers were in arms for their liberties? Did they not try to hold my own dear father on our plantation as hostage for a British officer of rank whom Colonel Marion captured in one of his daring raids, coming almost to the city limits? You ask for Roy; — he is out there, somewhere in the swamp, with his dashing leader, serving galiantly through hardships untold for the great and glorious cause of Freedom."

The fire of patriotism blazed in the hazel eyes as they flashed upon Geraldine, but the glowing blue ones flung back the challenge.

" You speak as you have been reared to do, and so will I. My duty and loyalty are for the king, whose faithful subject I am, now and always."

" Do you mean it?"

Rose's low cry of anguish smote Geraldine to the heart, but she went on calmly : " We will never mention this subject again: I would be false alike to my father and myself if I permitted it. Rose, dear Rose, forgive me."

"Farewell!" The lovely, laughing face was set in stern lines as the mournful word left her lips; slowly Rose stooped and kissed her friend on the brow. "The day may come when you, too, will know that love of country is an all-absorbing passion beside which kings and crowns crumble and decay," and before Geraldine had time to fully realize the significance of her words and action, Rose vanished across the threshold, and ere Geraldine could follow and detain her the sound of the chestnut's galloping feet reached her ears, as horse and rider sped down the road and were lost to view among the myrtle trees.

CHAPTER V

UNEXPECTED GUESTS

"Jupiter, tell your mistress that I await her presence in the drawing-room."

"Yes, Marse Colonel."

"And fetch the decanters of cognac and port at once, and see that Margot has the chambers ready."

"Yes, Marse Colonel," and Jupiter vanished as Colonel Moncriffe ushered his visitors with stately courtesy across the square hall and up the staircase into the drawing-room, whose wide door stood invitingly open to receive them.

"I crave your pardon for our somewhat untidy appearance," said Tarleton, throwing himself into an armchair as Captain Halleck followed his host into the room. "We stopped half an hour at the fort, leaving my troopers there, and trusting to Halleck's recollection for the road. My orderly is somewhat behind us; his saddle girth broke and we left him patching it up as we rode along."

"Your portmanteaux reached here yesterday," said Colonel Moncriffe; "Colonel Prevost sent them down by pack-horse, and one of my blacks will attend you gentlemen at your toilets. I think you will find him a clever valet, for I devoted some time to his training."

"I appreciate your kindness; faith, 't is so long since Halleck and I have doffed our uniforms that other clothes will set awkwardly upon us. What a fine mansion you have here, colonel," gazing around him at the costly furniture and carved pillars which divided the entrance to the hall; "I could fancy myself once again in London except for the clinging jasmine vines outside the window, and the mocking bird singing yonder in the thicket."

Colonel Moncriffe colored with pleasure. "You compliment me, sir: may I offer you a glass of cognac? What's that, Jupiter? I fail to catch your message."

"Yes, marse," said Jupiter, who with silver salver and glasses stood bowing at his elbow. "Young Missy begs you'll 'cuse her as she's occupied wid de young ladies dat come two hours ago, an' she'll hab de pleasure ob seeing de gentlemen later."

A quick frown passed over Colonel Moncriffe's face, but recovering himself he said with good humor, "I had forgotten our fair guests, Mistress Molly and Anne Durbeville, who have driven out from Savannah to join our party this evening. Gentlemen, I make my daughter's excuses, and will, if you permit me, escort you to your chambers." So with Jupiter following he led the way down to the right wing of the mansion, where

were the suite of rooms on the first floor known
as "bachelor quarters," and reserved for all un-
married guests.

At the first door stood Phœbus (the blackest
sort of darky, named after the Sun-god in a moment of satire by his master), and beside him a
droll little assistant in the person of Cupid, his ten-
year-old son, whose chubby face and rolling black
eyes instantly attracted the attention of the
guests.

" By Gad, you 're a knowing-looking specimen,"
said Halleck, unbuckling his sword and flinging
himself upon a couch which stood invitingly beneath the open window ; " here, boy, can you pull
off my riding-boots ? "

" Yes, Marse Redcoat," grinned Cupid, as he
saw his father perform the same office for Colonel
Tarleton in the chamber adjoining, whence presently came a sound of splashing water and other
evidences of the performance of a toilet. Halleck,
with Cupid's assistance, was proceeding in a leisurely manner to induct himself into a suit of
clothes which he had dragged from his portmanteau,
when there came a knock on the door of his room.
Cupid sprang to open it, and on the threshold
stood the trooper, Burt.

" Beg pardon, captain ; I came to report myself."

" Colonel Tarleton is in the next room ; anything the matter, Burt ? you look troubled."

" Nothing much, sir ; I have been thinking ever

since that Indian girl's escape that some scheme is afoot, — perhaps an Indian outbreak, — and I made bold to say as much at the fort."

"Afraid? eh?" Burt flushed, but a queer smile lighted his face as he shook his head.

"Not I, captain. But here on this plantation it would be an easy matter to capture" —

"Who talks of capture?" Tarleton's door was thrown open and he appeared fully dressed in all the bravery of satin and lace, with his hair powdered and tied in a queue, a strikingly handsome, elegant figure. "Is that you, Burt? What are you croaking about? Have you not found your quarters, or what's amiss?"

Burt saluted gravely. "I made bold to tell them at the fort of our adventure in the forest, and they'll post an extra sentry to-night, sir, in the direction of this plantation."

"Very good, you may retire," and Burt disappeared.

"I vow, Tarleton, you are in luck," said Halleck, with an envious glance at his friend; "how came you to essay powder? My ambitions had not reached that point, though I have put on ruffles," and he surveyed himself with an air of vast satisfaction in the mirror above the mahogany dressing-table.

"Sit down and let my black fellow arrange you," said Tarleton, laughing. "He seems a neat hand at a perruque."

"Bress de Lord, Marse Colonel teach me 'bout

dressing de hayd long time ago," said Phœbus, waving his powder-puff solemnly. " Cupid, you jes' stand an' hold de box, and obliterate de rug wif it," and while the much amused officer submitted to the hair-dressing operation, Tarleton walked up and down the apartment, his head bowed in deep thought.

Upstairs the mansion was the scene of busy preparation. When guests came to dine at Glenmoira, they and their horses and chariots were always put up for the night, and on this, the re-opening of the hospitalities of the family, every arrangement had been made in the most lavish manner. Margot, presiding with great dignity over a corps of black servants, detailed a maid to each of the different guests, reserving to herself and a bright, pretty mulatto girl named Ginger the delightful task of completing Geraldine's toilet. Well did Margot know what was in the wind of matrimonial possibilities, and mingled with her loving admiration of her young mistress was very decided disapprobation, which, however, she was sufficiently shrewd to keep to herself.

An hour later Geraldine stood beside her proud and satisfied father in the drawing-room as Colonel Tarleton was announced in a loud voice by Jupiter, who prided himself upon his sonorous accents on all social occasions. Profound was the bow and deep the courtesy with which the pair saluted each other, and Tarleton's dark, handsome eyes were fixed with admiration on the beautiful young girl whose hand he ventured to kiss in courtly fashion. Dressed entirely in white, with a shining train of satin, with her exquisite neck and bosom slightly veiled in lace, her hair guiltless of powder, and around her lovely throat a string of priceless opals (the gift of a princely Stuart to her grandmother), Geraldine's blue eyes smiled graciously upon her suitor, whose passionate, fickle heart went down before her beauty, and made her the one genuine love of his bold, reckless life.

The gay and brilliant company were handed out in the fashion of the day, the gentlemen conducting the ladies by their finger-tips. Colonel Moncriffe led the way with Lady Dolly Menteith, the sister-in-law of the commandant at the fort, and Geraldine followed with Captain Sir Charles Adderly, of the fleet now stationed off New York, who, in obedience to Sir Henry Clinton's desire to know the exact situation at Savannah, was making a brief visit to Colonel Prevost. Tarleton, to whom was assigned pretty Mistress Anne Durbeville, found himself seated at Geraldine's left, to his infinite satisfaction, and he proceeded to put all his power of fascination at work to interest the charming young hostess. But he soon found that it was no easy task to rivet her attention ; the blue eyes that were by turns so playful, mischievous and alluring, were also disdainful and a trifle haughty ; never had he seen so tantalizing a beauty, and as one witty story after another fell from his lips, and the conversation of the entire table uncon-

sciously turned to him, Tarleton vowed that "The
Blue Bell of Scotland" should be his, and his
alone.

"Do you know, colonel," said Lady Dolly
Menteith to her host, "I spent the time I was
driving out this afternoon in little thrills of excitement and with a cold, creeping feeling going
up and down my spine, fancying that perchance
I might be ambushed by Indians, or have some
wonderful adventure to carry back to England
with me as a reminiscence of my sojourn here."

"Indians!" said Molly Durbeville, at the other
side of her host; "you are more likely to suffer
from a raid of Marion's men. Good lack, they
have been more daring than ever of late; did you
hear, colonel, of the capture of Mr. Sylvester by
them as he was riding into the city? And it was
in broad daylight, too."

"They are a most daring rebel crew," replied
Colonel Moncriffe, "but you need suffer no appre-
hension, Lady Dolly, for I believe they confine
themselves to capturing men, and the fair sex has
so far escaped."

"But 't is deliciously romantic; why, one feels
quite like Hampstead Heath and 'stand and deliver,' highwayman fashion. Do these gentlemen
rebels demand one's purse and jewels?"

"At all events we will try to protect you from
having to answer your own question, Lady Dolly.
I cannot tell you what pleasure it gives me to see
you at my table and beneath my roof," said Colo-

nel Moncriffe, bestowing a glance of admiration upon the lady, who promptly resumed the coquetry for which she was famous.

"That was a maladroit remark," whispered Molly Durbeville to her right-hand neighbor, a young officer from the fort named Selwyn; "from being the dearest friends, I hear that our host has fallen out with Mr. Telfair, ever since the affair of the magazine, when that gentleman assisted the Whigs to carry off the king's powder."

"Is n't there a young Telfair who has joined the raiders recently?" asked Selwyn.

"Aye, Roy Telfair; so 't is said, but you know an atmosphere of mystery surrounds the whole thing. No one knows who belongs to Marion's force; he has friends and sympathizers everywhere. If it were not that your coat is scarlet I might even suspect you," and Molly laughed roguishly, in the ensign's face. "What think you of our young hostess? Is she not marvelously beautiful? We were playmates before she went to England, and no one was so great a favorite as she among us."

But Selwyn, with wisdom beyond his years, was careful in his reply, and the conversation between him and his teasing companion soon turned upon more personal subjects.

The dinner was nearly over, the cloth had been removed, and Colonel Moncriffe had proposed the health of his guest Colonel Tarleton in most glowing terms, and Tarleton rose to answer and to give the toast in return. Wine had flowed freely, and several of the men around the table were beginning to show its effects, but Tarleton, beyond a slight flush and perhaps added fluency of expression, displayed no trace of his cups.

"I am somewhat put to the blush," he said, "in responding to sentiments which are beyond the measure of my deserts. I have been for some four years a resident of these colonies, — colonies so fair that Great Britain cannot forego her claim to them. And not alone does the mother country desire to retain her lands, but her gallant sons and lovely daughters as well, who, though born on this soil, are still hers by descent and kinship. I drink, therefore, to our bewitching hostess, fair Mistress Geraldine, on this her home-coming after a three years' absence, and with this sentiment; To the American White Rose, and may she deign to smile on the pretensions of the humblest of her slaves, who wears the colors of the king," and bending forward with glass in hand Tarleton plucked a ruby rose from the vase before him, which he extended to Geraldine; but before she could accept or refuse it, it was snatched from his hand and a clear, calm voice, which rang distinctly out above the clash of glasses, said sternly, —

"Go seek your roses elsewhere! Gentlemen, you are my prisoners!"

Geraldine sprang to her feet and looked around the apartment. In each window and at the door stood armed men, — men in the motley garb of green and brown, but stern of face and with their guns leveled, as the keen eyes glanced down the barrels and waited for their leader's command, which followed swiftly.

"Protect the ladies — seize every man and secure him; let none escape."

With a fierce oath Tarleton rushed upon his captor, but powerful as he was he was unarmed, and in hand to hand wrestling was no match for the agile American. Panting and breathless with rage, his lace ruffles torn, and his satin coat stained with wine, he was placed in a chair, his hands bound behind him, while Colonel Moncriffe was struggling and shouting in despair at the other end of the room.

"Villains, thieves, murderers, how dare ye invade a man's house and insult his guests in this fashion! But you shall pay dearly for it; oh, I know whence you come. You are Marion's men, — that foul traitor who raids thus on innocent women, — and no doubt your leader can be bought, if the ransom be but high enough. Where are my slaves? Jupiter, Sambo, Phœbus, — will you see your master made prisoner thus — oh, villains" — and he sank almost speechless with wrath on the settle beside Lady Dolly Menteith, who began to sob violently.

"Here, good Master Robbers, take my jewels — my necklace, my bracelets — but spare my life, and let me but get back to Savannah in safety."

"Tarleton," shouted Halleck from the seat where he also was pinioned, — "where's Burt? Call, and perhaps he'll hear you."

"Gone to the devil," retorted Tarleton, furiously; "oh, for my sword; I'd soon settle you, sir," and he glared at the leader, who stood quietly beside him.

"I shall be at Colonel Tarleton's disposition at any time when the fortunes of war do not compel me to make him prisoner," was the stranger's answer.

The whole attack and capture had taken place with the greatest rapidity, and Geraldine, clinging with one hand to the table, in her first fright, cast her eyes rapidly about her, — the black servants had evidently been secured first, outside; she had not noticed that when the toasts began Jupiter and his assistants had withdrawn, and the entrance of the Rangers had been so skillfully planned that with every eye turned upon Tarleton no one had seen the unexpected guests. What could she do to rescue her father and their friends? Oh, for a chance to slip out and mount her horse — or should she make appeal to the leader, whose voice seemed strangely familiar? Where was Margot — where? But just at the moment that these thoughts were whirling through her brain, she felt some one touch her foot underneath the table, and the start and exclamation she gave passed unheard amid Lady Dolly's screams, and the general hubbub which prevailed among the guests, for every one was talking, the ladies crying, the men swearing, and the only silent ones were those grim Rangers in green. Looking down cautiously, Geraldine saw peeping out, beneath the mahogany table, a small woolly head and the rolling eyes that could only belong to Cupid, who, for some purpose best known to himself, had carefully hidden there before the dinner began, fallen asleep, and only waked at this very exciting moment.

Geraldine was quick of wit; with a sudden movement she contrived to overturn the massive candelabra which with its wax lights stood on the table before her, and as the cry of alarm sounded through the room (which was rendered dim for the moment, though not entirely dark), she bent down as if to gather up her train and seized Cupid by the arm.

"Quick, crawl on your hands and knees to the pantry window — drop down to the ground from it, and fly up the road to the fort for help."

Frightened, but still capable of obedience, the boy crept along under the table, which extended nearly the length of the room, and once at the end, it was easy for him in the confusion which the rolling candles had made to escape observation and find the pantry door. Cupid was an adept in climbing trees for bird-nesting purposes, and had often received chastisement at the hands of his mother for indulging in that pastime ; therefore he slid down from the pantry window by a catalpa tree with the agility of a monkey, and in three minutes more was tearing along the avenue, dodging in and out of bushes, and making for the road which led to the city.

CHAPTER VI

"Whist, mon, are ye there?"

It was a very low, soft whisper, and Margot crept along cautiously in the dark passage connecting the servants' quarters with the house. On the brick floor lay the figure of a man, evidently bound, for just before she spoke he had been endeavoring to roll himself along nearer the door which opened on the porch; but at her whisper he lay still, and answered with equal caution : —

"Who are you?"

"I've come to let you free of your bonds; those above" — mysteriously — "told me when I heard an owl hoot beneath the willow you were to be freed," and stooping down she cut the band which held his arms and legs, with a knife which she concealed behind her. "I'm thinking that knot was na drawn over snugly," she said, with a grim smile; "perhaps like some ithers ye are not precisely what you seem."

"Hush," said Burt, as he regained his feet, "give me your knife — I've a part to play as well as you," and snatching it from her he felt his way in the dark to the door, behind which he crouched as Margot departed silently as she came.

Above stairs the uproar and confusion which had attended the capture of Colonel Moncriffe and his guests was beginning to subside. Geraldine drew back from the table, where she had made her daring attempt to assist Cupid's escape, and in the dim light she saw the Rangers lead their prisoners out of the door, and knew by the sound that they were being taken down the staircase. The ladies rushed after their respective husbands and friends, sobbing and imploring, except Lady Dolly, who was indulging comfortably in hysterics on the settle, and Molly Durbeville, who endeavored to compose her. Geraldine gave a terrified glance around, and then flew through the open door.

" Father, father, where are you ? " she cried, sudden terror getting the better of her as she realized that perhaps he was being borne from her, and frantic thoughts rushed through her brain of what Marion might deem fit reprisals for the indignities heaped upon the Whigs of Savannah. But as she reached the stairs the tall figure of the leader barred her passage.

" Stand aside, sir," she ordered haughtily ; " do you forbid a daughter to seek her unfortunate parent ? "

" You will not find him below ; in accordance with my instructions we have left Colonel Mon-

criffe safely bound in his own chamber.   No harm
is intended him, and beyond a few hours of dis-
comfort he will be none the worse."

"I shall release him at once."

"Not while I hold the key of his door."

"Give it to me instantly, sir; how dare you
commit such an outrage!" and for the first time
Geraldine raised her eyes to the handsome face
above her.

"Roy!" The girl staggered back a step, and
caught at the balustrade for support.

"Geraldine!" He stretched out both hands
toward her, but she shrank farther away, growing
deathly pale as she gazed.

"And so we meet again," she murmured; "so
I find you — in arms against your lawful king,
invading a peaceful home, imprisoning my guests.
Oh, God! can it be you, my playfellow, my" —
She choked for breath; a dry sob left her lips.

"Your lover," cried Roy Telfair, passionately,
"aye, your lover still.   Do you think I have
forgotten one sweet word you spoke" —

"Hush, sir, for shame's sake; do not dare to
remind me of that day.   You have forfeited every
right to — to — my friendship, and I forbid you
to remember anything."

On the stillness of the night outside the mansion
there suddenly broke a distant sound of a bugle,
and close below the window near which the pair
stood came the "hoot — hoot" of a night owl;
with a swift bound Roy Telfair darted down the

stairs, and Geraldine, gathering her gown in her
hand, fled after him. In the darkness of the
porch she could dimly discern a band of mounted
men some of whom evidently had their prisoners
before them on the saddles, and directly in front
of the door stood a horse apparently waiting for
its master. To this animal Roy Telfair bounded,
catching the bridle of another horse, which stood
beside it, on whose back, well secured, Geraldine
saw a figure which she recognized as Colonel
Tarleton. Quick as a flash she darted forward
and seized the rein, and Roy pulled his horse
almost back upon his haunches to avoid trampling
upon her as she stood directly in the path.

"Are you mad? Let go that horse, I implore
you," cried Roy. Again the sound of a bugle
floated on the wind, — this time nearer, — and
standing in his stirrups Telfair shouted to his
men : "Disperse !"

Like shadows, and almost as silently (for the
horses' feet had been muffled), one by one the
Rangers faded from view, and, stooping down,
with a supreme effort of strength he lifted Geraldine from the ground and swung her before him
on the saddle. But the gallant feat was just too
late, for as Roy seized the rein of Tarleton's horse
from her hand, there came a rush of troopers up
the avenue, a shout from Tarleton, " This way,
men, quick, quick ! " — and in another moment
they closed around the group, and the brave young
Ranger was in the hands of his foes.

"Pursue those fellows for a rescue," shouted Tarleton, as his men dragged Telfair from his horse and helped Geraldine to the ground; "send half the force in pursuit, keep the others here with me. Is that you, Burt?" — seeing who was releasing him from his bonds, — "by gad, you were just in time, my brave fellow, and shall be rewarded." Burt smiled grimly at the mistake, but did not think it wise to enlighten him, and he assisted Tarleton up the staircase, as the colonel was somewhat cramped from being bound to the horse.

"Into the library," said Tarleton, "and tell them to fetch the prisoner here," and while Burt departed with the order, he endeavored to adjust his coat and ruffles which had become disordered in the scuffle, and to compose his face into its ordinary calmness before he heard the approaching footsteps of his prisoner.

"And now, sir," he said, throwing himself back in a chair, as two troopers brought Roy before him, "I think the tables are well turned, though the result may not strike you as satisfactorily as it does me. Who are you, and for what reason did you commit to-night's glaring outrage?"

"My name is Roy Telfair, captain in the Georgia Rangers, commanded by Colonel Francis Marion of the Continental Army."

"One of the lieutenants of the Swamp Fox! Well, sir, proceed."

"There is no further reply necessary," said the

prisoner calmly; "I have nothing to explain. Colonel Tarleton has probably heard of reprisals, and after his most dastardly conduct to our wounded at the battle of Waxham Creek, should expect nothing less at the hands of an American officer."

"Then, Captain Telfair, as you know me so well, you will not be surprised by my ordering you shot at daybreak," said Tarleton, with mocking courtesy that was the more cruel because of its suavity. "You dared to lay hands upon Mistress Moncriffe, the lady whom I have the honor to address in marriage, and your ruffianly conduct shall meet its deserts. Ah, you grow pale, sir; the prospect of meeting one's deserts is not always agreeable to contemplate."

"I shall not stoop to argue with you, but let my execution take place outside the bounds of this plantation, in common humanity to those whose guest you are."

"I require no lessons in courtesy, sir. Go!" To the troopers, — "Keep the prisoner in close confinement until I send the order; find some room below where you can bestow him," and as the men conducted Telfair from his presence, Tarleton started to seek his host.

The rescue by the British had followed so swiftly upon her fruitless attempt to detain Roy that Geraldine, as soon as her feet touched the ground, paused not a moment, but flew up the staircase, and met Margot on the gallery.

"Oh, Margot, did they seek to harm you? are you unhurt? And my father — we must release him at once. He is in his chamber, bound"—

"No," said Margot, laying a detaining hand upon her mistress's arm, "the colonel is below; dinna ye hear him?" as the sound of remarkably fluent and forcible English oaths sounded from the porch. "I made bold to enter by your room when I heard the din the colonel was raising, and"—

"But Roy had the key — oh, Margot, it was Roy, *Roy*, who dared execute this bold outrage, for which I will never, never grant him forgiveness."

"Hush, hush, my bairn; we are come upon troublous times, and it does na become me to advise ye, but auld woman that I am I have still to see the day when a human being could dare assert that she wad be mair implacable than the Almighty."

They were standing near the door of Geraldine's room, and just at this moment glancing down they saw the troopers bringing the prisoner up the staircase. Pressing back into the dimly lighted gallery they watched the group enter the library.

"Margot," whispered Geraldine, "go down to the door, stand without and listen, and fetch me word here what Colonel Tarleton says to Captain Telfair." The woman nodded, and went softly around the gallery as Geraldine opened the door of her own room.

"Oh, 't is you at last," cried Molly Durbeville,

from the couch where she had thrown her pretty
self; "we thought the Rangers had carried you off
among the others, and I was about to set forth on
a hue and cry after you when Anne dragged me in
here."

"Where are the others?" asked Geraldine; "I
must look after Lady Dolly and the rest."

"You need not; Lady Dolly is safely bestowed
in the blue chamber with Ginger for company and
guardian; the others Margot has taken care of,
and we have invaded your room because, forsooth,
Anne, here, was so terrified that I thought between
us we might beat some composure into her timid
pate."

"Indeed, indeed," sobbed Anne, "I am confi-
dent Mr. Selwyn will be hanged or murdered"—

"Or drawn and quartered! Was ever so silly
a maid as you? Marion's men do not commit
murders — they are our protectors and defenders.
Surely you cannot accuse Roy Telfair of belonging
to any cut-throat crew?" said Molly, with vehe-
ment indignation.

"Roy! Do you mean to say he was there?"
and Anne's curiosity effectually quenched her
tears.

"Had you no eyes? Why, he was the leader
who snatched the rose from Colonel Tarleton's
hand — Oh, Geraldine, that was neatly done. And
did you hear the challenge that passed between
them?"

"I did not know that it was a betrothal dinner," said Anne. "Your father has kept the secret well."

Geraldine wrung her hands. "I entreat you, say no more. That Colonel Tarleton honors me by his addresses I acknowledge, but the matter has not yet been decided, and" — she paused, the bright color which had flown to her face died away to almost ashen pallor as she saw Margot open the door.

"Will you step here, my leddy," said Margot, drawing Geraldine outside and closing the door behind them. "It's ill tidings I bring ye, and ye must act swift and sure if ye wad save a life. Maister Roy dies the morn; he's to be shot at daybreak."

Geraldine's beautiful eyes filled with horror. "Shot!" she gasped; "no, no, it shall not be!" She flew down the gallery, Margot following swiftly after, and as she reached the door of the library she almost fell in to Tarleton's arms as he issued from the room.

"I crave your pardon," he cried, with his winning smile; "I was just starting to find your father and inquire for your well-being."

With intuitive quickness Geraldine seized the situation. "I am unhurt, and came to ask if you are the same. Can you spare me a few moments, Colonel Tarleton? Margot, await me here," and with almost perfect self-possession and calmness she crossed the threshold, and sinking into a chair motioned Tarleton to another.

" I cannot tell you how deeply I am grieved that you should receive such treatment at the hands of my misguided countrymen," she said softly. " You will have most unpleasant recollections of your first evening under our roof."

" On the contrary, it would require more than the raid of a few outlaws to obliterate the remembrance that I have not only had the happiness to sit beside you and gaze upon your beauty, but I feel that to your brave effort on my behalf I owe my rescue."

" You are pleased to flatter me ; I perceive that Colonel Tarleton knows how to compliment."

" Compliment ? ah, madam, never have I seen such courage as you displayed in seizing my rein, helpless as I was, and the act is engraved upon the heart of Banastre Tarleton. You know what brought me hither; my high hopes, my ardent aims. It is, perhaps, too soon to say all that is in my mind, but here at your feet I lay my devotion."

" Stay, sir, stay ; I had not meant to provoke this avowal, and mayhap it is not quite maidenly to see you thus without my father's presence. But I heard that you were here with a prisoner, and my womanly curiosity prevailed so far that I came to ask who and what he is ? "

" He is not worth your consideration ; a pestilent fellow, named Telfair."

" Telfair ? the son of my father's old friend and neighbor ? "

"The same, probably," said Tarleton carelessly, his eyes still fixed upon her in admiration. "I think he called himself Captain Roy Telfair, of Marion's men."

"And what disposition have you made of him? My father will be grieved to know of his disloyalty."

"He is under guard below, somewhere, but where matters little. He dies to-morrow; let us talk of happier things."

"Dies!" Do what she would, the color fled from Geraldine's face. "Colonel Tarleton, you shock me beyond words. Oh, sir, do not, I beg you, begin our acquaintance in this manner; it were an evil omen," and she shuddered violently even while she courageously lifted her eyes to his.

"Forgive me," he answered gently. "I am but a bluff soldier and unused to the softness of women's hearts. I should not have told you so abruptly."

"Nay," she said, with an enchanting smile, while every nerve in her body thrilled with terror; "nay, grant me his reprieve. It would sadden me too much to feel that you pronounced sentence against one whom I have known in childhood's days."

Tarleton looked at her keenly, but subtle as he was he could not penetrate behind that smile; he did not know that the hand which waved her fan had crushed its delicate sticks until they broke.

"An old play-fellow?" he questioned lightly.

"Yes, and no. Rose Telfair, his sister, and I were old and dear friends; I suppose she will hardly speak to me now that I am so loyal to the colors of the king."

Tarleton threw himself on one knee and kissed her hand. "The queen — *my* queen commands," he said gallantly; "what is a miserable rebel's life, after all? Take it; it is yours."

CHAPTER VII

ROY'S REFUSAL

THE troopers who conducted Captain Telfair below found Burt at the foot of the stairs.

"What's to be done with the prisoner, O'Brien?" he asked of his comrade, a happy-go-lucky Irishman, who was a great favorite among the men.

"Faith, it's a short shrift," answered O'Brien, with a compassionate glance; "shot at daybreak. Sure, what did ye expect?"

Roy, alert as ever, caught the whisper, and looking at Burt, saw something in his face which gave him a ray of hope. He had no intention of submitting tamely to untoward fate, and was ready to take advantage of the slightest chance for his life.

"The colonel's orders are to confine him closely; any place will do."

"Then follow me," said Burt, turning down the passage which led to the servants' quarters, where he had been rescued from his bonds by Margot; "there's a storeroom here which has bars across its only window, no doubt for keeping out the blacks, who are a thievish lot where provisions are concerned. It will do excellently, as you have only to turn the key in the door and keep guard outside."

The light was dim in the passage, as it came from two tallow dips stuck in a pewter sconce, one of which Burt took in his hand as he opened the storeroom door. The soldiers peered curiously about, but all the narrow room (scarcely more than a closet) afforded was rows of shelves either side of the barred window referred to, and a floor flagged with brick and stone like the passage. On the shelves were jars of jellies and conserves, dear to Margot's housewifely soul, and packages of tea and coffee, with sundry blue jars of quaint shapes which evidently contained condiments and delicacies pertaining to the table.

" I shall not starve," said Roy with a smile, as he surveyed these; "get me a stool and a bit of writing paper, and I 'll ask for nothing more."

" Hold him fast till I return," answered Burt, sticking the candle in a cup which stood conveniently on a shelf. He was back in a second, and producing a scrap of rather soiled paper from his pocket, set down the three-legged stool which he had procured from his own quarters.

" Here 's your seat," he said somewhat roughly, for O'Brien's eyes were upon him, and O'Brien was almost as keen as Burt himself. " The paper is not very clean, but it 's all I have," shaking it open to prove that nothing was written upon it ; " d' ye wish to write a letter ? "

" Perhaps," returned Roy, and then his eyes

lightened, for, as Burt passed the paper into his extended hand he saw a very faint tracing in one corner of an Indian arrowhead.

" Come on, men, we 'll not disturb him longer," said Burt, turning hastily away as he perceived he was understood ; " sleep if you can ; you 'll be called, never fear," and they filed out, O'Brien locking the door and taking the key carefully out of the lock.

Half an hour after Jupiter came slowly along the passage blinking like a venerable owl, and evidently in a state of agitation. Attacks and rescues were decidedly out of Jupiter's line, and he was more frightened than he ever had been in his life. Consequently when his eyes fell upon the soldiers stationed at the door of the storeroom, and saw the guns standing against the wall, his teeth began to chatter and he imagined he should be seized and punished.

" I ain't don' any harm, please, good massa-raid-coats ; jes' comin' ter look for de colonel's gem'-man. Dun' no what yo' call 'im, but he 's de one who comed dis evening, befo' dinner, — befo' de battle."

" Battle ! " said O'Brien with a grin ; " save yer sowl, d'ye call that race a battle ? More by token our fellows should be reportin' before long, though I have me doubts if all the followin' in the world would catch up wid them thieves of Rangers. It 's fleet heels they have, an' sorra a wan of our officers will we see till they 're exchanged or ransomed, I 'm thinkin'."

" Whar am de gem'man? " said Jupiter, obsti-
nately standing his ground, though trembling,
" caise I 's got a message fur him from de raidcoat colonel."

" Why did n't you say so? " sharply; " do you
mean the prisoner ? "

" Dun no nuffin' 'bout prisoner, marse; I was
tole to find de raidcoat who come down on de portico when yo' was dere."

" He means Burt, the colonel's orderly," said
the other soldier.

" Oh, aye, Burt; well, here he comes," for the
door at the end of the passage swung open at the
moment.

" Dun yo' hear dat bell ringing? Dat 's yo'
colonel," turning to Burt, " an' he says he wants
yo' to fetch de prisoner straight up to him."

" Whew," whistled O'Brien as he put the key
in the door; " wonder what 's to pay now ? Hope
he is n't going to attend to that little matter which
was coming off at daybreak with his own hands."

" It would n't be the first time if he did," muttered Burt to himself, his heart beating a trifle
quicker as he tried to imagine what new turn
affairs could be taking.

Roy looked up as the men entered. " It 's not
daybreak yet," he said calmly; " can I not be left
unmolested until then ? "

" You are wanted above," said the Irishman,
catching him by the arm and motioning to his
comrade to take the other side. " I say, Burt," in

a whisper as they moved down the passage, " d' ye think he's having a change of heart? It's a foine young fellow we'll have to shoot."

"Hush," said Burt sternly, and in silence the little group marched up the stairway, Burt saluting at the door of the room.

"The prisoner is here, sir," he said.

"Bring him in, close the door, and let the others stand guard outside."

Roy crossed the threshold with firm step; if he felt emotion of any kind as his gaze fell upon Geraldine leaning back in her carved chair, it did not appear in his face as he bowed haughtily to Tarleton, quietly ignoring her presence. A faint flush mounted to Geraldine's cheeks, but she toyed with her broken fan, and dropped her eyes until the long dark lashes almost hid them from view.

"I have sent for you, sir," said Tarleton, in coldly polite tones, " to change somewhat the order with which I dismissed you a short time ago. This lady"— with a wave of his hand toward Geraldine — "has been pleased to intercede for you."

"I am deeply indebted — to the lady," returned Roy, with a profound bow.

"In response to her request I have decided to remit your sentence of death, and shall hold you close prisoner at the fort to await the orders of Sir Henry Clinton. Well, sir, have you no word of thanks for my clemency?"

"I beg to congratulate Colonel Tarleton upon experiencing so novel an emotion. Faith, unless the lady vouches for you, sir, it will hardly be believed."

"You go too far, sir; you go too far," cried Tarleton, springing from his seat, his face convulsed with sudden passion; "it is not yet too late to return to my former mind as regards your affair." As he spoke, his coat, which was still somewhat disordered from his hand-to-hand conflict with Telfair, fell open, and from his breast rolled a small case, which, breaking as it touched the highly polished floor, landed at Roy's very feet, disclosing the miniature portrait it contained of Geraldine.

Tarleton darted forward, but ere he could reach it, Roy had seized the picture. With one long, eager gaze he took in every detail of the lovely face; then he laid it in Tarleton's hand.

"I return your property," he said courteously, "with an apology for unwittingly seeing what was not intended for my eyes. You have offered me my life at Mistress Moncriffe's intercession. I decline to take advantage of her well meant, but wholly unauthorized effort on my behalf, and prefer that Colonel Tarleton should follow his natural impulses undisturbed."

"Captain Telfair!" Geraldine's voice fell unheeded upon his ear. In the wild passion that possessed him, Telfair was, for the moment, beyond the bounds of reason.

Tarleton darted a quick glance of keen suspicion at the pair. Telfair regarded him with a contemptuous smile, while Geraldine, with the spirit and pride of her gallant ancestry, would have died rather than have betrayed to either man the agony they were causing her.

"You hold your life lightly, sir, and are either a desperate man or a very brave one. Notwithstanding what you are pleased to call my 'natural impulses' I can find it in my heart to admire your recklessness. Remove the prisoner, Burt, and see that he is well secured."

Everything swam before Geraldine's eyes, and it was only by an intense effort of will that she controlled herself sufficiently to acknowledge Roy's salutation as he turned and left the room, and she sat motionless while the sound of his footsteps died in the distance.

"On my word, the gentleman has a taste for raising my temper," said Tarleton, with a light laugh; "he is somewhat of a dare-devil to provoke me thus."

"I trust, Colonel Tarleton, that you will not permit his — his — I scarcely know what to name it, — his behavior, to affect your decision?"

"His insolence," interpolated Tarleton quickly. "Madam, my word is pledged to you, and Captain Telfair shall have his life to throw away as he pleases after his release from captivity in British prisons, which, if I read Sir Henry Clinton's mind rightly, will not be soon. I have the honor to kiss your very beautiful hand and to thank you for the boon of this interview."

With trembling fingers Geraldine accepted the salute, and swept from the apartment to find Margot in the gallery. But at the touch of Margot's hand her forced composure forsook her, and throwing her arms around her old nurse's neck she burst into a passion of sobs and tears.

Burt had scarcely obeyed his orders and locked the door of the storeroom upon Roy Telfair before he was summoned to Tarleton's bedroom. The colonel had thrown off his coat, and was writing rapidly. Burt stood at attention and waited his leisure.

"Here," said Tarleton, signing his name to the paper, and dusting the ink with sand from a box at his elbow; "I cannot spare the others, so you must take horse at once and speed to the fort with this for Colonel Prevost. The night is too far spent for any arrangement at daybreak, but noonday will serve as well." The last sentence apparently escaped him unawares, for he cast a penetrating glance at Burt as if to see whether it had been heard, but that worthy presented a perfectly stolid countenance as he saluted, turned on his heel, and left the room; and Tarleton, undressing with great rapidity, flung himself upon his bed and was presently fast asleep.

Burt went down the passage and made his way outside; he eyed the note with much perplexity as he passed the lantern which swung in the portico. All was still inside; after the rush and excitement every soul seemed to have retired. He paused, glanced uncertainly into the darkness, then wheeled and stole cautiously back to the portico, where he carefully unfolded the note intrusted to him. It took but a moment to master its contents, and Burt swore under his breath and shook his fist as he read.

"'T is as I suspected. Oh, wily villain, to make smooth promises one moment and belie them the next," he thought rapidly. "How to circumvent him! If I could find the woman who cut the cords for me when I lay bound yonder — has she gone to bed as well as the blacks? I have it; I must ride dispatch on the colonel's business, and I 'll be hanged if I know where to find my horse without assistance," and back went Burt, softly as a cat, into the house. "She was there at the door waiting for the young mistress; I 'll warrant I 'll find her somewhere in the gallery." Step by step Burt went up the staircase, and his shrewdness was rewarded, for his foot had not touched the topmost step when he saw Margot, candle in hand, emerge from Geraldine's door, and he heard her bid "good-night" as she closed it behind her.

"Weel, mon, what brings ye here?" asked Margot, recognizing him as she reached his side. "Dinna make a noise, but let this distracted household sleep in peace."

"I want my horse," said Burt, in a tone that might reach a possible eavesdropper. Then in her ear, "Quick, follow me below if you want to prevent more deviltry than has occurred already."

"Come outside and I'll turn ye in the direction of the stables," said Margot readily, as she led the way down. "Ye are free frae listeners noo; what's your will?"

Burt leaned closer, as they stood under a myrtle tree before the door, and whispered rapidly. Margot started back. "D'ye mean it? Oh, the wickedness of man! Whist, let me think; in whilk room did ye put the prisoner?"

"In the storeroom; it has a barred window. He could not break it without noise that would betray him, nor could I help him from the outside without detection."

"In the storeroom! then 'twas the finger o' the Lord wha guided ye. Trouble your head nae mair; leave it to me."

"If you would be pleased to explain" —

"Tut, mon, and for what? He's safe, I tell ye, and dinna seek to know mair o' the secrets o' the house. What your brain does na ken your lips will never tell." And before Burt could lay hand on her, Margot disappeared in the darkness, and Burt, with a low chuckle of delight and amazement, went off to find the stable and his horse.

In the mean time, Roy Telfair, with wildly beating heart, was sitting in his narrow prison consumed with jealousy, love, and anguish. It was not enough that Geraldine — his mistress, his star of hope, the idol of his boyhood — that she should stoop from her high estate and ask reprieve of Tarleton,

but to know her false, alike to him and to her
country, — for what was he to conclude from
seeing that Tarleton carried her portrait in his
breast, apparently with her knowledge and consent? What indeed, except that every word of
love that had passed between them was forsworn,
that she was fickle as she was fair! Oh, God,
how beautiful she was, as she sat there, in her
pallor and distress. Could it be that even then
she repented; that she bethought of the vows
exchanged that day beneath the myrtle trees,
when she was about to put the ocean between them? She was very young, barely turned
sixteen, scarcely more than a child, and yet with
the depth of feeling and devotion of a woman.
Could it be that wealth, adulation, and the
flatteries of a court had changed her thus? Perhaps she had not known or fully realized the
momentous question of freedom and liberty for
which her people were fighting. Would it come
home to her heart some day? — But, no; there
was a gleam of satisfied ambition in Tarleton's
eye; his air of proud proprietorship could not be
mistaken. Well, it would soon be over; a volley,
a shot, and — He hoped they would give him
decent burial. And then he turned his face to
the wall, and thought of his father, — his grand,
noble father, who had given all to his country, —
and of his sister Rose, and his brave heart swelled
almost to bursting.

How long he sat thus a prey to agonizing

reflections, Roy never knew. The tallow dip was
burning low in its socket when a very faint noise,
like the scratching of a mouse, attracted his attention. He looked up in its direction, and
noticed that a blue jar which stood upon one of
the shelves shook a trifle, as if it had been stirred.
He wondered if the mouse might be inside; then,
as he fixed his eyes upon the jar he became con-
scious that a crack in the wall which he had not
perceived hitherto was widening before his eyes.
Fascinated by this curious phenomenon he watched
for a moment; slowly the crack opened, the shelf
moved back, and Roy beheld a hand silently beck-
oning to him, and behind the hand a face he knew,
— the face of Margot.

Despairing lover though he was, the desire to
live was by no means extinguished in Roy. Very
softly, step by step, in order that his movement
should not be heard by the guard outside the
door, he drew near the narrow aperture which the
panel disclosed, and bending his head he finally
passed through it to the other side. Margot took
his hand, and slowly, without even a creak, the
panel, under her skillful touch, swung back to its
place.

"Creep after me on your hands and knees,
Maister Roy; after a few rods you may stand up
again," whispered Margot in his ear.

Roy obeyed, and after proceeding several feet he
felt the air of the vaulted passage rush higher over
his head. By a pressure of his hand, which she

still retained after he rose to his feet, Margot pre-
served his silence; then they went on for a short
distance, when another turn brought them to four
steps, up which they mounted; and Roy found
himself in a good-sized room, around which he
glanced with a look of recognition as the lantern
placed on the floor enabled him to see his surroundings.

"The old summer-house!" he exclaimed. "Why,
Margot, I never knew of the existence of this
underground passage connected with the mansion."

"It's no likely ye would, Maister Roy; the
mistress confided the secret to me nine years syne,
and somehow I never saw my way clearly to
informing the colonel."

"Then no one knows but you?"

"An' yoursel'; mind ye keep the secret. Had
it not been for my getting the word in time ye
wad dree the weird that yon bloody colonel has
planned for you. Nay," for Roy threw his arms
around her neck, and kissed her fondly, "dinna be
foolin' wi' an auld wife like me. Get ye gane,
and take better care o' yoursel' in future, for if ye
fall into British hands after this night's work it
will gae hard wi' ye."

"Not harder than this has been," said Roy,
bitterly. The Scotchwoman looked at him with
shrewdly affectionate eyes as she laid her hand on
his shoulder.

"Dinna take too much for granted; there's
mony a deed planned whilk never reaches matu-

rity, and mony a heartache whilk a bit o' patience
will explain away," and giving Roy a gentle push
outside the door of the summer-house Margot
walked rapidly back to the mansion.

CHAPTER VIII

ROSE'S DILEMMA

IT was early morning, and the mocking birds were whistling in the thickets at Dumblane, as Rose Telfair stepped lightly out on the verandah which ran across the south side of the mansion and was raised a few feet from the ground by brick pilasters. Without possessing the stately air of Glenmoira, the place had an attraction of its own in its peculiarly fine old trees and wealth of vines, the latter covering every available wall, and even the great brick chimney, which, being built on the outside of the house, was a picturesque feature of itself. A Virginia creeper, with a mass of scarlet blossoms, climbed up one side of the verandah and was met by a wilderness of morning-glories, that joined hands with the creeper in its laudable achievements and reached the slanting roof overhead. As Rose leaned over the railing and looked out in the sunshine, she sang gayly a snatch of the old Jacobite song : —

> " Fling open the West Port and let me gae free,
> For 't is up w' the bonnets o' Bonnie Dundee ! "

" A good morning to you, fairest and most rebellious of cousins," called a voice from below, as a

young man in a riding-suit emerged from behind a
tall china tree; " you are late this morning."

" Not I," returned Rose, " 't is you who are
early. Who gave you permission to invade Dumblane at this hour?" saucily; " I am sure it was
not my mother — for she is still in her chamber, and
I recollect your bidding me a most serious, not to
say solemn, farewell two days ago when I met you
in the city."

" If you did not look so enchantingly pretty
peeping out between those scarlet flowers I should
feel inclined to mount and ride back to the city,
even without the breakfast that I came for," said
Allastar Murray. " Give me at least a blossom to
pin in my coat to console me for your unkindness.
You have no idea how scarlet becomes you; ah,
you must return to the colors of the king at last."

With a provoking smile, Rose turned and
plucked a lovely blue morning-glory from the vine
and tossed it down to him. " Be it upon your own
head, sir; if you wear my flower it must be one
of rebel blue, whether it suits with your humor
or not."

Murray caught the flower as it fluttered from
her hand. " Rose," he said entreatingly, " how can
you "—

" I will even come down and pin it to your
breast," quoth the willful coquette, as she gained
the steps and ran swiftly down them. " Here,"
with a pretty air of command, and standing with
her head on one side as she surveyed his perplexed

countenance; "nothing ever looked so well in your buttonhole as this."

"If you would not make everything a matter of partisanship "—

"Very well, sir," coldly, "you can scorn my gift if it pleases you to do so."

"Oh, Rose, Rose, pin it on at once."

"You know you began it," returned his tormentor, as she finally adjusted the offending blossom to her satisfaction, and stood with her hands demurely folded, contemplating the effect of her teasing. "So you came over to breakfast with us? I fancy Dinah has had it smoking hot this half hour, for I confess I am somewhat tardy. I was later than usual in returning last night."

"Then you were at Glenmoira? I heard that Colonel Moncriffe was giving a large dinner to celebrate the home-coming of his daughter."

"No," answered Rose, her eyes suddenly filling with tears, as she discreetly dropped them from his view. "I was bidden to that feast, but I — declined."

"And wherefore? Surely you are not so prejudiced as to refuse to welcome an old playfellow and friend because the men of your families are at variance over a political quarrel?"

"Precisely so; you are beginning to understand me at last."

"Nay, I think I am farther from it than ever."

"I saw Geraldine yesterday; she is more beautiful than she was, if that were possible, and my heart was filled with joy to see her once more. But — Oh, talk of something else; my mind is weary with these endless dissensions."

"A truce to them," said Murray gently, as they turned toward the door.

"Hark, what is that?" asked Rose, as the patter of running feet struck her ear, and looking around she saw flying up the path the chubby figure of a little black boy. "What ails the pickaninny? He seems decidedly out of breath," said she, as the new-comer brought up before her, panting with his exertions. "Who are you? and what do you want?"

"I 'se Cupid," said the image, and stopped for breath, rolling his eyes in a most comical manner.

"Shade of Eros!" ejaculated Murray; "where has he left Psyche?"

"She 's home, marse," said Cupid, with an air of surprise; "laws, do yo' know my sister?"

"Do not tease the child — I think he is frightened. Cupid? oh, aye, you are one of the pickaninnies from Colonel Moncriffe's. I recollect you took my horse yesterday when I was at the plantation."

"Yes, missy, I 'se Phœbus' boy, an' I come to tell yo' we had mighty wild times las' night. De ladies an' gem'men was to dey dinner; an' somehow rudder de green Rangers bust in de doors and winders, an' when I waked up under de table dey was shootin' and firin', an' Missy Geraldine, she jus' took de candles an' frowed 'em round de

room, an' she ketch me by de arm whar I was onto
de flo' by her feet, an' whispers I 'se to get out de
pantry winder an' run fur help to de city;" and
Cupid, exhausted with his own eloquence, sat deliberately down on the ground at Rose's feet.

"The Rangers!" gasped Rose; "I can scarce
believe it. Go on, Cupid. What did you do
when your mistress told you to seek assistance?"

"I croup 'long under de table, an' slipped down
de catalpa tree 'longside de winder, an' I ran, an'
I ran, up de road like de hounds was after me,
an' 'bout halfway to de city dere was a redcoat
soldier, an' he caught me, an' scared me mos' to
deff wid he gun, an' I tole him whar I come from
an' how my mistress sent me for help, an' he called
a lot more o' dem, an' dey all rode back to marse's
house."

"Another raid of Marion's men! What happened then, Cupid?"

"I sat down on the roadside, an' I reckon I went
fas' asleep, 'caise when I waked up de sun was
shining, an' I jes' come long hyar an' stop by for
something to eat, 'caise I 'se mighty hungry, I is."

"Dinah will give you breakfast. But, Cupid,
tell me, how did you know it was the Rangers? and
was any one hurt when the guns went off?"

"I 'se seen dem befo'," said Cupid, with a rogu-
ish twinkle in his eye. "I come on two ob dem
one day when I was hunting up de river for birds'
nests, an' dey was good to me — dey gave me silver
money to carry a letter inter dey city, an' I jes'

stuck it in de winder whar dey tole me, an' ran away fo' anybody ketched me."

"He is n't Cupid, he 's Mercury," said Murray, unable to help laughing at the imp's face and manner. "Do not look so terrified, Rose; the story is somewhat incoherent. I 'll wager there was not a gun fired. Here, Cupid, did you see anyone shot?"

"No, marse, but I see de Rangers holdin' up dey guns an' lookin' like dey was boun' to shoot mighty quick, an' two ob dem was tying ole Marse Colonel to de chair, an' de ladies was screaming — all 'cept Missy Geraldine."

"Rose, Rose," called a gentle voice from the verandah. "What are you and Allastar talking about? I have been trying to tell you that breakfast is ready, but you pay no attention."

"Oh, mother, such news; we 'll be with you in a trice. Cupid, go and find Dinah and get something to eat," and Rose, followed by Murray, went into the dining-room, where Madam Telfair had preceded them.

She was a commanding-looking woman in the prime of life, with silvered hair and soft hazel eyes, and her manner to her kinsman was full of graciousness, although she knew how widely apart the gulf stretched between Whigs and Tories. Allastar Murray was a far-away cousin of her husband's, who had come to Savannah from Scotland just before the War of Independence broke out, and had shown his fondness for kingly rule by

affiliating with the Tory society there, having been
private secretary to the governor of the province,
Sir James Wright (upon his return to the city in
1780, after its capture by the British), and he
still held the position, greatly to the annoyance of
Rose, who took every opportunity to tease and torment him upon his political principles. But as
Murray had been hopelessly in love with her ever
since they first met, he could find it in his heart
to forgive her for being a staunch Whig, and perhaps (though he would not admit as much) the
young Scotchman loved her all the more for her
enthusiastic patriotism.

The Telfairs were among the most highly re-
spected families in the province. When the news
of the battle of Lexington reached Savannah,
Edward Telfair, with five others, had secured a
large quantity of powder stored in the king's
magazine, and secreted it so carefully that although
a reward of one hundred and fifty pounds sterling
had been offered for its recovery, it was never
found, but was actually sent North and used at
the battle of Bunker Hill. Belonging also to the
Council of Safety, Rose's father stood high in the
confidence of the Whigs, and being made a dele-
gate to the Continental Congress, was, at this time,
in Philadelphia, having left his wife and daughter
upon the plantation in charge of his son. But
after the siege of Savannah, Madam Telfair could
restrain her boy no longer, and Roy cast his lot
with Colonel Marion, whose bravery and untiring

energy in pursuit of the British appealed to the gallant young Southerner's very soul. The fact that Rose and her mother remained alone with their black servants at Dumblane afforded sufficient excuse for Allastar Murray's frequent visits there, and his position with Governor Wright enabled him, in a quiet way, to obtain both favors and protection for them which were not often vouchsafed the Whigs, especially since the cruel and stringent rules of the British officers had obtained in Savannah.

When Rose had finished telling her mother Cupid's story, the ladies looked at each other, an unspoken terror in their eyes. What if Roy had been one of the daring band! He had sent them a message two days before, and therefore could not be far away. Indeed, so sudden and unexpected were Marion's raids both in South Carolina and Georgia that it might easily happen that Roy would appear at Dumblane at any moment. But Rose, after giving her mother a reassuring smile, proceeded to keep up a running fire of mischievous and teasing questions, as much to cover her unspoken anxiety as for the pleasure of tormenting her cousin.

" What is the news in the city? It seems you have to come to Dumblane to hear what is going on, even if only one of the Swamp Fox's raids. I am dying for some bit of gossip. What are you doing at the governor's house, for example?"

" Making ready for a fête which takes place

shortly, in honor, Sir James tells me, of Mistress Geraldine Moncriffe. Lady Dolly Menteith is to play the part of hostess, and it promises to be a grand affair."

" Lady Dolly is rather a gay young dame, is she not ? " asked Madam Telfair.

"Oh, aye, but so playful and amiable that she makes herself a great favorite. I am sure my cousin Rose would find her a most agreeable companion."

" Your cousin Rose is not in a way of seeing much of her at present. And how are the Durbeville girls ? Anne, no doubt, fainting at sight of a mouse, and Molly speaking her mind without regard to tact or policy."

" Which is very descriptive of another than Molly," said her mother with an indulgent smile. " I thought we heard somewhat of the devotion of one of the officers at the fort to Molly."

"You mean young Selwyn; 't is a pretty boy, but hardly worthy bright Mistress Molly."

" Protect me from my friends," cried Rose. "Are not you and Mr. Selwyn bosom companions ? "

" Surely, there is nothing opprobrious in my remark ? He is but a boy, and he is "—

" Pretty ! " with a pout of scorn, " oh, whatever a man may be — Why, Hector," to the servant behind her mother's chair, " what are you about ? You will certainly drop that coffee cup if you flourish it so wildly."

" Yes, missy," returned Hector. " Somebody have come to see you," and he pointed toward the open window. As he did so, a shadow fell on the floor, and looking behind her quickly Rose saw in the doorway, upon the threshold, the slight figure of an Indian girl.

" Laceola ! " Rose sprang to her feet, with outstretched hands. " How glad I am to see you ; it seems long since you were here."

" The White Fawn's words are sweet," said Laceola, stepping inside the room ; " her voice is like the running brook which plays in the sun. Laceola has walked many miles since sunset, but she forgets the long road when the White Fawn speaks."

Murray looked up in surprise at the girl's musical voice and poetry of speech.

" Have you never chanced to meet Laceola ? " asked Madam Telfair. " She and her brother, Ossaba, wandered to our door after the battle with the Creeks some years ago, when Ossaba was a lad of fifteen and she about ten years old. We took them in, fed them, and taught them English, but we never have been able to induce Laceola to remain with us. The brother and sister belong to the Musgogees, one of the tribes of the Creek nation, from which the chiefs are taken ; and when you look at the girl it is easy to imagine her possessed of royal blood among her own people. The totem she wears is the symbol of her rank ; Ossaba has the same tattooed upon his left arm.

Rose taught her English, but the poetic rendering of her Indian similes is all her own."

"The White Fawn's eyes are troubled; perhaps Laccola can say some words to make her dream pleasant things. Can Laccola speak without fear?" and the girl shot a quick glance toward Murray.

Rose gave the slender hand she still held a warning pressure. "Have you come from the Enchanted Mountain?[1] Is not this the time of year when the tribes meet there?"

"Not yet; Laccola has been with the Uchees. Their squaws are on Isla Island, not far from the place called 'the stone of help.'"

"She means Ebenezer, the German settlement," said Rose. "But the British soldiers are there now. Laceola, you must be more careful how you wander through the forest."

"No one dare harm Laceola," said the Indian girl haughtily. "She carries a knife and can guard herself. But the White Fawn must eat; when the sun has come an hour higher in the sky, Laceola will return and talk with her."

"No, no!" cried Rose, perceiving that Laceola's visit meant more than appeared upon the surface. "Come out on the verandah with us and we will 'powwow.'"

"No time for 'powwow,'" shaking her head with a smile; "the wild pigeon flies in the day;

[1] A mountain so called by the Indians of that day because of the curious natural formations upon the rocks found there.

when night falls she perches in the trees out of
reach, where the hunter cannot climb, but the
bounding elk stays on the plain below."

Rose's heart gave a throb of dismay. "The
Bounding Elk,"— that was Laceola's playful name
for Roy; was he in danger? She must let the
girl execute her errand in her own way, trusting
that Murray would not understand the gravity of
the situation or Indian hyperbole.

"Let the Wild Pigeon fold her wings and rest,"
said Rose, readily adopting the simile; "she can
both eat and drink here."

"She drank from the brook where the water
flows clearest in the spring-house," returned
Laceola, bending a penetrating look upon her.
"The tramp of horses had muddied the stream
below."

"Horses? Did you ride around through the
plantation as you came this morning?" said Rose
to Murray.

"Not I," he replied carelessly, as he rose from
the table; "probably Cupid's friends, the troopers,
may have taken the short cut through this place to
reach Glenmoira."

"Very likely;" and Rose, Laceola, and Murray
stepped aside to permit Madam Telfair to pass
through the door, but the Indian girl made a sig-
nificant gesture unseen by the others as she whispered in Rose's ear, "The Bounding Elk waits at
the stream — go quickly," and then she glided
with noiseless step on the verandah.

Rose stood motionless for a moment as she realized her dilemma. Roy must be concealed at the spring-house; he might even be rash enough to come to the mansion unless she forestalled him, and Laceola's words convinced her of the necessity of haste. She dare not trust to Murray's sense of kinship if he were suddenly confronted with one of Marion's men, and beside, his confidential position with the governor might be jeopardized were it discovered that, in addition to his frequenting the plantation of such well-known Whigs, he had met a rebel in arms there. What excuse should she make? how absent herself long enough to fly down to the spring-house without suspicious rudeness? For twit and tease him as she might, in her heart she had rather a good opinion of Allastar Murray's quickness and ability, and that added to her ardent desire to outwit him in the present emergency.

There was but one thing to do, and Rose promptly executed her little plan. If she could induce Laceola to tell one of her Indian legends she could slip off quietly during the recital, leaving her mother to listen and take care of Murray. And fortune favored her, as that fickle jade does sometimes when we least expect it, for when she followed the others to the verandah she overheard Murray say, —

"What a singularly musical name — even for an Indian."

"Laceola? Yes, is it not? You should hear

her tell the legend, and why she bears it. For it is not a woman's name, is it, Laceola?"

The girl looked up at Rose, and divined her meaning, for she threw herself on a cushion at Madam Telfair's feet, and began her tale in her low, monotonous tone which somehow had a strain of sweetness and pathos in it.

"Laceola was a brave chieftain," she said proudly, "and because I am of his blood, I bear his name. Long ago before the pale faces ever set foot in the land of my people, and the Indian walked his native forests, there lived a moon's journey from here the beautiful Nacoochee. She was the daughter of the chief of her tribe, and many young braves sought her. But one day, wandering alone in the thicket, an arrow sped so closely that it grazed her arm. She cried aloud in terror, and the bushes parted, and a young brave glided softly toward her. Nacoochee knew by his totem that he belonged to a warlike tribe who were enemies of her father, and prepared to die. But struck by her beauty and helplessness, he kneeled at her feet, confided to her that he was Laceola, the chief of his tribe, and binding up her wound begged her to forgive him. It was enough; the young blood flows fiery in the veins of my people, and from that moment they loved each other."

At this point in the story there arose a sound of voices from the dining-room. Laceola cast a beseeching glance at Rose, who sprang up, seeing her opportunity.

"That is Hector arraigning Cupid for some piece of mischief. Go on with your story, Laceola; I will return in a few minutes," and sighing with relief, as she blessed Cupid in her heart for his pranks, Rose flew down the staircase and out of the back door, down the path to the spring-house.

Laceola resumed her story with unruffled composure. "After that day Nacoochee was changed. Every day the lovers met by stealth, and the young chiefs and braves of her tribe became despairing, for she would not smile for them. At last, one spring day her father followed her, with several of his young men, and concealing themselves in the thickets saw the lovers' meeting. Filled with rage, he fitted an arrow to his bow and drew it upon Laceola, but Nacoochee's keen ears had caught the sound, and as she flung herself upon Laceola's breast, the arrow found her heart. Then the chief and his companions fell upon Laceola, and so, pierced with several arrows, still clinging to Nacoochee, he died. But the Great Spirit was angry because of the slaughter of two unoffending lovers, and He caused remorse to fall upon the chief, and they were buried in the same grave, and a great mound was made to mark their tomb. That lovely valley where they died is called Nacoochee to this day, and Laceola goes sometimes to invoke their spirits to aid her when she is sad." [1]

Rose fled like a lapwing through the still wet

---

[1] For this legend, see *Historical Collections of Georgia*. The Nacoochee Valley is celebrated for its beauty.

grass, and as she reached the spring-house her heart beat almost to suffocation lest she was too late. But as she ran up the steps, a dear voice spoke softly, and in another instant she was clasped in her brother's arms.

"Oh, Roy, Roy, is this prudent, is this wise? If 't was you of whose raid last night I heard, you should have been many miles away in the forest. Every instant here is a fresh danger."

"Hush, Rose; do you think I would have left my command willingly? No, I have been tasting the fruits of captivity — almost of death, — and but for dear old Margot I might now be looking down the muzzles of the guns of a squad of British troopers detailed to shoot me for my treason."

"Good God," she gasped, "how, and wherefore?"

"Because I have had the ill luck to fall into Tarleton's hands."

"Aye, he was expected at Glenmoira last night, so Geraldine told me."

"Geraldine!" he said bitterly; "never name her to me again. She is false to the very core; troth-plighted to him, that monster of cruelty."

"Oh, Roy, indeed you wrong her. She is not yet plighted; she told me" —

"I tell you I saw the love-token, her miniature; it rolled from his breast on the floor, at my feet, and she did not gainsay it. She asked him for my life, Rose, and I flung it back in his teeth, and for a time I believe I went utterly mad."

" You are not yourself now; I do beseech you to be calm, and fly before it is too late."

" Nay, I renounce her — and henceforth I live but for my country. Alas, my mind misgave me when she left her home. I might have known that a woman cannot withstand the glitter and glamour of a court, corrupt though it be, or the questionable gallantries of a man like Banastre Tarleton."

" Roy, be still." Rose laid a small, firm hand on his arm. " Somehow I cannot quite believe you. When I looked in Geraldine's eyes yesterday there was the same steadfast beauty as of old. She avowed her Tory principles, and I left her in momentary anger, for you know my spirit cannot brook an enemy to my cause or my country. Be not rash; try to see, when your passion cools, that there may yet be a chance " —

" And you think I would take it? Surely, you cannot understand what you propose. Never, Rose, never! Farewell; my duty to my mother, and all the love I have left to you both. Tell Laceola to follow me to the Swamp; she knows the place. Farewell, farewell! " and leaving a fond kiss on her upturned face Roy dashed down the steps, crossed the brook, and was gone.

CHAPTER IX

IN MARION'S CAMP

ON the banks of the Ogeechee River, some thirty miles from Savannah, and as the crow flies, nearly opposite the settlement of Ebenezer, there was a level plateau of perhaps a quarter of a mile, when you emerged from the forest, and, troubled with comparatively little undergrowth, continued on to a bluff, below which ran the stream, making a sharp bend as it flowed southerly. Generally speaking, this plateau was silent and deserted as the rest of the forest around it, save for the deer that came to drink there, but this morning it was full of unwonted visitors and presented a scene of busy activity. Picketed to the live-oak trees were full sixty horses, whose riders were busy giving their beasts food, and then leading them, one by one, to the shore to drink from the river, while at a campfire other men were broiling fish and game, preparatory to breakfast, which would soon be ready.

On top of the bluff, overlooking the water, were a group of men, who, though they bore no insignia of rank on their green blouses, were unmistakably the officers of the detachment. Brown of face, sturdy of limb, they looked like genuine sons of the forest, and one could almost fancy himself back among the bold outlaws of Robin Hood's band, who fought, as these of a later day and new-born colony, for freedom from the tyranny of an English king.

"It strikes me, McKay," said a young fellow, not more than twenty, who was peeling the bark off a willow stick which he had just broken to use as a riding switch,— " it strikes me that we should hear something of Telfair and his expedition. What good fortune it will be if he contrive to capture Tarleton! And why should he not, as he had certain information that the colonel was moving southward with a few men as escort? I confess I envy Telfair his detail," and he heaved a genuine sigh of regret.

"Wait until you hear the result. Telfair may have met with unexpected obstacles, and the rendezvous is not until to-night, here, at this spot. Gad, if he does manage to capture 'the butcher' he will be the most to be envied of any of the Rangers; for I know Colonel Marion burns to avenge the slaughter at Waxham Creek."

"And well he may," cried the youngster fiercely; "'Tarleton's Quarter' is become a by-word and the rallying cry to us, one and all."

"What's that?" said McKay, springing to his feet, as his quick ear caught the sound of breaking twigs in the thicket to the left of the plateau, and following the sound they saw an Indian glide toward them, waving his hand in apparent amity and good faith.

"Ossaba, the scout, — news then," and off sped McKay to where the leader stood with his trusty lieutenants around him.

" The Rangers are coming; they bring ten prisoners to the Swamp Fox," said Ossaba, gravely saluting Marion, who stepped forward to meet him.

" Redcoats?" questioned he briefly.

" Two; others all city men; much eat, much drink, much 'fraid, like squaws — ugh!" said Ossaba contemptuously.

"Two, only, — if by chance one should be Tarleton!"

" Not big chief; Bounding Elk tie him to horse — then come redcoat men and seize Bounding Elk: Ossaba hide in thicket; Rangers ride away."

" By heavens, gentlemen, he means that Telfair is in the hands of the enemy, and that enemy may be Tarleton himself. God forbid that our expedition should end thus disastrously," and Marion's bronzed face grew pale at the very thought.

" Hark, here comes the detachment," cried McKay, as the sound of voices, mingled with the movement of mounted men seen through the trees, reached their eager ears, and the troopers appeared on the plateau, and flung themselves off their tired horses, while the sergeant in charge dismounted and made his report.

"Just arrived from Colonel Moncriffe's plantation, sir, with ten prisoners, captured while at dinner by Captain Telfair. No casualties, but have to report the captain as captured by a squad of British troopers, who came suddenly upon us as we were about riding off. Captain Telfair had taken Colonel Tarleton with his own hands, and had him securely tied to a led horse, but being hampered by Mistress Moncriffe's appearance and by her throwing herself directly in his pathway, he ordered us to disperse, which order we instantly obeyed, and Captain Telfair was captured."

" Better have lost the prisoners than have consigned Telfair to such fate," cried McKay passionately.

" The sergeant seems to have obeyed orders," said Marion quietly, as he saw the color brighten in the trooper's cheeks. " Where are the prisoners? Fetch them before me at once." McKay bit his lips, and as Marion saw the hot tears that rushed to his eyes, he said in a low tone, " Trust Telfair to extricate himself if possible ; if not, we may effect an exchange."

Colonel Marion, with his officers, stood confronting the prisoners as they were grouped before him, guarded by the Rangers. They presented a somewhat woe-begone appearance, with the exception of the two officers, Major Sefton and Ensign Selwyn, while Sir Charles Adderly had lost his débonnaire air of elderly beau, and with his queue untied and his lace ruffles torn was a prey to the

deepest dejection. Having been treated by the
Tories to tales of ferocity and bloodshed regarding
Marion and his men ever since reaching Savannah,
he did not for a moment suppose that the courteous, almost mild-mannered gentleman who addressed him could be the famous partisan leader of
the South.

"May I ask your name and rank, sir?" said
Marion, saluting him gravely.

"Captain Sir Charles Adderly, Royal Navy,
commanding His Majesty's ship Hornet, now
stationed in New York harbor."

"And how came you off duty, sir, in Savannah?
Perhaps for a pleasure trip?"

"I have hardly found it such in this portion of
His Majesty's dominion, I do assure you. I am
ordered here by Sir Henry Clinton, to report the
condition of ships in the port of Savannah and
the state of feeling in the province toward the
crown."

"I fear that the latter is not such that you can
report favorably," said Marion dryly. "Stand
aside ; who are these officers?"

Major Sefton and Selwyn now came up for inspection, and after asking them a few questions he
dismissed them, and then Marion confronted the
remaining seven others.

"So," he said sternly, " we have here a group of
men of whom I know something. All of you, save
one, are men of means and education, born on this
soil, the sons of those who came to these shores to

find that greatest gift of God, freedom of speech and action. And how have you used your privileges? — traitors that you are to your kin and neighbors, who open your homes to the soldiers of a corrupt king, who come to curtail our liberties and to force us to adopt unjust laws at the point of the sword! Answer for yourselves, if you can, for at the door of such as you lies the blood shed at Charleston, at Waxham, and at the siege of your own city of Savannah, which cries to Heaven for succor."

The American Tories stood mute under Marion's fiery arraignment; hardly a man dared meet his scornful eyes, and after a moment's pause, to control his passion, Marion resumed.

"You will be taken, securely guarded, to my camp in South Carolina, there to remain until I can exchange you for men who are now imprisoned in Charleston. I will see that messages be sent your families in Savannah as to your condition as prisoners of war. Guards, remove the prisoners."

As Marion was about to turn away and seek his breakfast, he perceived Ossaba standing at his elbow.

"Ossaba has more to tell the Swamp Fox," said the Indian softly. "He heard the redcoats talk as they fed horses; Ossaba lie still, listen; they say Bounding Elk will be shot at fort; big chief very angry with him."

"When? — did you hear when?"

" No, Ossaba hear too much talk; too many tongues same time." Marion stood for a moment in deep thought; then he walked back where the two English officers were seated beneath a tree, eating with apparent relish the breakfast of broiled fish that had been set before them.

" I have received intelligence which somewhat alters my plans in regard to one of you two gentlemen. Your name, sir, I think you told me, was Selwyn ? "

" Yes," answered the young man, springing to his feet and unconsciously according to Colonel Marion the courtesy of a salute.

" Then I wish to ask if I release you upon parole to carry a message from me to your commandant, Colonel Prevost, will you deliver it and keep faith with a Whig and a rebel ? "

A flush stained Selwyn's cheek. " Why not, sir ? Although the British consider your command in the light of outlaws, I am aware that you hold a commission from the so-called Continental Congress, and therefore I accept parole."

" I thank you, sir; my message will be brief, but you will see that there is need for speed in the matter. I am informed that Captain Telfair, who commanded the detachment which made you prisoner, has been condemned to death by Colonel Tarleton. You will kindly convey to Colonel Prevost my assurance that I hold Captain Sir Charles Adderly as hostage for Captain Telfair, and that so surely as harm befall my comrade, Sir

Charles's life will answer for it.   You understand
me, — his life.   A horse here for Mr. Selwyn ; you
will pardon my cutting short my farewell, as I am
aware that Colonel Tarleton acts with dispatch,
and I advise you to make the best speed you are
capable of.   Ossaba my scout will conduct you on
the trail as far as the town of Ebenezer; when
there you can readily reach Savannah.   Farewell,
sir, and recollect that two lives hang on your
speed."

Marion walked hastily away, and in less time
than it takes to tell, Selwyn found himself again
mounted on horseback, and with Ossaba in close
attendance, plunged into the forest on his return
journey to Savannah.

CHAPTER X

THE household at Glenmoira slept late the morning after the dinner which had been so rudely interrupted by Marion's men, and Venus, chief of the kitchen, had sent two messages to Jupiter before that worthy appeared, rubbing his eyes and full of apologies for oversleeping.

" Such goings on," sniffed Venus, her red madras handkerchief poked ominously over her left eyebrow, as it was given to be when her temper was ruffled. " De bes' sort o' sweet puddin's and cheese-tarts all los', de salads frow'd onto de pantry flo', and ebery 'ting topsy-turvy 'caise dem rebels come here invadin' peaceful folks. An' de quality too. I 'd like ter know what Marse Colonel and young miss hev got to do wif dem ole green-coats ; de raid ones is much mo' to my mind, I jist tell yer dat, Jupiter."

" Dun no 'bout dat," quoth Jupiter, with a dubious shake of his grizzled pate. " Did yer 'preciate de fac' dat de young marster who grabbed de rose outen de British colonel's han' was Marse Roy, Madam Telfair's son an' Missy Rose's brudder ? He come 'long up de staircase jis' as I was 'bout fetchin' marse de ole an' bes' port, an' he clap him han' on my arm an' says, ' Jupiter, my ole fren', don' yo' interfere in dis 'fair,' an' he march me down de stairs, like a lamb, an' turns de key on me in de twinklin' ob an eye, an' dere I stay till yo' come and let me out.''

" An' yo' was hollerin' fit to raise de daid," returned Venus, beating eggs vigorously. " Why, in de Lord's name, did n't yo' do dat befo' ? "

" Befo' ? " asked Jupiter with an air of injured innocence, " what fer I go spile sport dat er way ? "

" Call dat sport ? You 'se a mean sneakin' ole Whig, dat 's what you is," snorted Venus, who had long since declared her preference for kings and Tories, " an' yo' ought to be 'shamed o' yourself, wif yo' gray hairs, helpin' such spoilin' ob good food an' spillin' ob good wines ! Hi, who dat comin' bawlin' and cryin' into my kitchen, I 'd like ter know.''

In the doorway appeared the distracted figure of a young slave girl, closely followed by Phœbus, who seemed to be doing his best to comfort her.

" It 's only me an' Cinthy, Aunt Venus. She cayn't fin' Cupid, an' she 's certain suah dat de rebels done carry him off wif dem.''

" He 's daid, he 's daid, my lil' Cupid," wailed Cinthy. " I hear de whipporwill cry free times behin' de wood-pile night fo' las', an' dat 's heap bad luck, an' I 'll never see my chile no mo'," and she threw herself down on the floor with an evident intention of developing hysterics.

"Stop dat," said Aunt Venus, setting the eggs down and seizing the girl with a firm hand; "dey 's no use o' yo' makin' a fool o' yo'self 'fo' yo' know de chile ain't somewhar 'roun' de plantation. Dem rebels ain't spendin' dere time huntin' fer piccaninnies. 'Caise dat boy is smart an' peart, ain't no reason fer makin' dem dare-debils any blacker dan dey is. Yo' jis' stop yo' nonsense, Cinthy. I 'clare fer it, ef Phœbus cay n't make yo' behave I 'll jis' call somebody who can."

As Cinthy knew that this threat meant an appeal to "marse," whose temper was of the shortest, and to whom a piccaninny more or less only signified as they were valuable for his purposes, she thought better of giving way to hysterics, and was presently consoled by Phœbus' promising to ransack the entire place in search of the missing one, and a cup of Venus' hot coffee proved successful in stopping her tears for the time being.

"Dar goes marse," said Phœbus, as the sound of a gong came echoing down the stairway. "Reckon he ain't 'pearin' in de shape ob an angel dis yer mornin', an' be keerful, Venus, dat de coffee am clar an' strong."

"Yo' go long an' min' yo' own business, an' lemme 'tend to my cookin'. What *am* dis plantation comin' to when de niggers tink dey can specify Venus' coffee!"

Phœbus dodged the egg the insulted goddess of the kitchen sent whirling at his head, and subdued his chuckle over having teased the divinity as he rapped cautiously on Colonel Moncriffe's door.

"Here, boy, fetch me my morning punch," came the voice behind the curtains of the four-posted bed, "and be quick about it. Have my guests arisen?"

"I tink not, marse, ain't heard any ob dem stirrin' 'roun' in de bachelor quarters," said Phœbus, bringing the decanter from the dresser to the bedside, and pouring out a glass of its golden contents. "Marse Captain was mighty lucky las' night."

"What captain, you rascal? Oh, I suppose you mean Halleck, the gentleman who arrived with Colonel Tarleton."

"Yes, marse, de way was dis. When de Rangers "—

"Damn it, boy, call them rebels."

"— Rebels," corrected Phœbus submissively, rolling his eyes as he went deftly on with his master's toilet, "when dey fotched all de gem'men out an' perceeded ter put dem onto de hosses, de feller leadin' him foun' dat particular hoss what was fer him an' de captain was limpin' in de fo' foot, an' so he had ter stop an' see what's de matter, an' befo' he quite tended to dat foot de bugle was blowin' an' de British was hyar, an' so dat rebel jis' made off in de dark, leavin' Marse Captain on de groun'. He lay dar cussin', caise I hear him when I come 'long from de quarters whar I was locked up, an' I ran an' foun' a knife and cut de cords mighty quick. 'Pears like he was lucky, marse. Does you b'lieve dose prisoners will be shot by de rebels, eh, marse ?"

At this point Colonel Moncriffe relieved his mind by language which added to Phœbus' opinion that his mood was far removed from the angelic, and so impressed him with the necessity for speed in the toilet operations that the colonel descended to find his guests before the hour struck, and as he reached the portico there arose the most extraordinary hubbub in the region of the servant's quarters, and O'Brien came running out, breathless and frightened.

"Good-morning, sergeant," said Moncriffe, as the trooper paused, uncertain which way to proceed ; "are you looking for Colonel Tarleton ?"

" Yes, sir. I beg your pardon, sir, but are there ghosts in this house who can open doors without saying by your lave ?"

" Ghosts ? It 's early in the day for you to be drunk, my man," said Colonel Moncriffe in an offended tone.

" I 'm not drunk, sir, but small blame to ye for thinking so. I 'm on the way to report to Colonel Tarleton that the prisoner has escaped."

" Escaped ! "

" Yes, sir ; divil a bit of him can we find anyhow. We locked him in that storehouse beyant, the three of us, Burt, McGinnis, and me, and the bars at the window are not touched, nor disturbed, but the young gentleman is not to be found inside,

and we are ready to swear that we kept good guard
outside the door in the passage, for not a wink of
sleep came betune our eyelids the blessed night —
or what was left of it, for dawn was not long
coming after Burt rode off."

"But it's impossible — out of the question!
That storeroom has no exit except by the passage
where the servants' quarters are located. Are you
very sure you secured the lock properly?"

"Ay, sir," said the trooper doggedly, "an' not
a fly or a mosquito even could pass the keyhole
widout my knowing it. I'm told that witches
sometimes are seen on the plantation."

"Damnation!" Colonel Moncriffe's irritation
was beginning to find vent, when his colloquy was
ended by the appearance upon the portico of both
Tarleton and Halleck, the former laughing heartily
at some joke he had just been relating, when he
caught sight of his host.

"You look disturbed, sir," was Tarleton's greet-
ing as they bowed with stately politeness to each
other. "I trust your daughter and the other
ladies are well this morning and suffer no ill effects
from the drama enacted last evening? Had our
Ranger friends but given us intimation of their
purpose we might have rehearsed the play more
smoothly."

"I have not heard from our guests as yet, but
— pardon me — we have a more serious affair here.
Your sergeant informs me that the prisoner you
secured last night has escaped."

" What, sir ? " Tarleton's brow clouded and his dark eyes sparkled ominously, as he turned them upon O'Brien, who shrank back as he realized the fact of his colonel's anger. " Are my fellows capable of such loose guard as this? Speak, O'Brien, what 's occurred ? "

O'Brien in as few and terse words as possible repeated his statement. Tarleton thought for a moment and then his face cleared.

" So the beggar got away," he said with a laugh, greatly to the surprise and relief of O'Brien. " As I gave him his life when I dismissed him, the escape is not of much consequence; we are but a prisoner the less. But I own my curiosity is aroused as to the manner of his evading us. With your permission, Colonel Moncriffe, I 'll inspect the room where he was confined."

" With all my heart. I 'll accompany you, for 't is as much a mystery to me as to you."

O'Brien held open the door of the passage and they walked quickly down it. The storeroom stood open. McGinnis, gun in hand, leaned against the wall beside it, and back of him, huddled in a frightened group, stood Jupiter, Venus, and half a dozen other house-servants, all agog with surprise and terror.

Tarleton crossed the threshold, and taking the candle offered him by O'Brien, ran his keen eyes about the narrow room. But although he peered at each shelf, and felt along the wall on both sides of the window, he could discover no trace of any means of escape (so cleverly was the secret passage concealed), although he noticed a few drops of tallow adhering to the lower shelf. But that might have fallen from the cup which held the candle if it had been carelessly moved. He then stamped upon the floor several times; but as it gave forth no sound, he abandoned the idea, with a shrug of his shoulders.

"It seems a case where outside help was absolutely necessary," he said, addressing his host, "unless Captain Telfair has sworn a compact with the devil and been released by a thunderbolt."

"Telfair!" interrupted Colonel Moncriffe, "I do not comprehend you. I heard you had been so fortunate as to capture the leader of the band, but I did not hear his name or personality. Do I understand you to say it was Telfair? Not Roy Telfair!"

"Ay, sir, so he proclaimed himself. A son, I think, of some neighbor of yours." Tarleton checked his speech suddenly. He did not choose to inform her father of his interview with Geraldine, or the fact of her plea for the condemned captain.

"By heavens! there must be some collusion with my household," cried Moncriffe furiously. "If I detect my slaves at such tricks it will fare ill with them. Jupiter!" The old servant came forward. "How's this? Who is accountable for this outrage?"

"Dun know, no mo' 'an de daid, marse,"

answered Jupiter, the picture of injured innocence, and being, moreover, perfectly convinced that some supernatural agency had been at work, and that the hand of the Lord was assisting the Whigs, which was proof conclusive that they were His chosen people, " 'cept it 's de witches, or de han' o' Providence."

Colonel Moncriffe hit him squarely with a cane he carried. "None of your absurd nigger superstitions ; go question every one on the plantation, whether man, woman, or child were seen about outside the mansion after the troopers left, and report to me."

As he spoke, the blacks, who had been slowly sidling off down the passage, disappeared, and there came the sound of rapid hoofs nearing the door.

" Shall we see who comes ? " he said, addressing the two officers, and they retraced their steps in time to see Burt fling himself from the saddle at the portico.

" I delivered the letter to Colonel Prevost, sir," he said to Tarleton. "There was no reply, but the colonel's wishes should be followed in every respect, and they would be ready for the prisoner."

" The prisoner," said Tarleton, laughing, but with a sneer that sounded ominous in Burt's ears, "the prisoner has taken what we may call ' French leave.' "

" Shot himself ? " gasped the trooper.

" No, escaped ; though how, or by what agency

of this world or the next, opinion seems to be divided."

Burt recovered himself as he drew up in salute, and it was well that he did, for the sudden flush which covered his face caused Tarleton to bestow a glance of surprise upon his orderly which put Burt on his guard instantly.

"You're not suspecting O'Brien, sir?" he asked, with warmth. "You might as well suspect me, — and a damned sight better," he added to himself.

"No, no," said Tarleton, disarmed at once, for by a singular chance he felt a certain attachment to his quick-witted recruit. "Go to quarters, Burt, and after breakfast report to me. We will try other means to penetrate this mystery."

While this scene was transpiring below, the occupants of the several guest chambers were waking, dressing, and chatting with the respective maids detailed to assist them in making ready for breakfast. Lady Dolly, after her cup of coffee, which she had besought almost before opening her eyes, fell to lamenting her box of cosmetics which she had carelessly left behind in the city, and was only consoled by finding in response to a message that Anne Durbeville could supply the want, having just received a consignment from Paris by the last ship which came out to Savannah. But notwithstanding all the noise and chatter which penetrated the gallery, and even reached her chamber, Geraldine slept on, having just at dawn yielded to exhaustion and sunk into such deep slumber that Margot went twice to her bedside and forbore to wake her.

Margot had returned for the third time, and was about to draw the curtain, when with a sigh the girl turned on her pillow and awoke.

" Is it morning, Margot? oh, why did you suffer me to rest so long? Judging by the sun on my window the day must be advanced, and I must bestir myself to attend my guests."

" No such haste," said Margot, pouring water from the ewer and making ready for Geraldine's toilet; " the other leddies are still in their bedchambers, and the colonel has eno' on his hands for the present in cross-examining every black on the plantation ; hech, I 'm thinking he 'll even gang down to the rice-fields in his hunt."

" What has happened now?" asked her mistress in a trembling voice, as she thrust her bare feet into delicate fur-lined slippers; " surely one such unhappy night is enough for this household."

" Weel, I 'm thinking a knowledge o' events will na worry ye," returned Margot, with a twinkle of her eye. " It seents that when you redcoat troopers went to open the door o' the storeroom whaur the puir young prisoner was confined, in order to take him intil the city, he wasna there ; by some strange interposition he had clean disappeared."

" Gone — escaped? for Heaven's sake, how ? "

" Hoo' can I tell ye, my leddy; when your

father, the colonel, speers an' speers, and ca's all
the blacks to witness, an' not a trace to be found
o' Maister Roy's flittin' — wad ye suppose auld
Margot could be wiser than her betters ? "

" Margot ! " Geraldine caught the Scotchwoman
by both arms and her blue eyes beamed with sudden laughter. " Margot, look me in the face ; do
you mean to tell me that you had no hand in the
matter ? "

" I canna say wi' positiveness na, an' I wadna
be willing to proclaim yes. Is it not sound Bible
doctrine as expounded in the Kirk that ye maunna
let your right hand know what your left hand
doeth ? "

" You dear darling old casuist ! " Geraldine
gave way to her laughter, — laughter brighter and
more girlish than any that had passed her lips for
many a day. " You mean that if I ask you no
questions you 'll tell me no lies ; is that about the
state of your canny Scotch mind ? "

" Just aboot," said Margot, the twinkle broad-
ening into a smile, " an' if ye wad see to it that
Colonel Moncriffe will na pit me in the witness-
box, it wad be greatly to the relief o' ma conscience."

" Margot, Margot, no Jesuit ever evaded questions more cleverly. Be sure I am dying of curiosity, but I know you well ; when you close your
mouth in that fashion I — wait till to-morrow,"
and Geraldine's light-hearted laughter rang out
again. Then soberly, but with dancing eyes,

" Good Margot, to bring me tidings that my old playfellow has escaped a British prison.   It grieved me sorely to think of dear Madam Telfair and Rose's misery, and though Colonel Tarleton gave me the reprieve most graciously, I am more rejoiced, perhaps, than a loyal subject of His Majesty should be to feel that it is not under our roof that a rebel meets with his deserts."

Margot had it on her tongue's end to remark that possibly she did not enjoy a monopoly of Jesuitism, but she only said —

" Ah, my leddy, it always warms the heart to think we 've done a guid action, an' yours last night will perhaps bring ye mony a happy hour that now is hid frae your e'."

A beautiful bright blush dyed Geraldine's fair cheek, and she moved away lest the kindly, shrewd eyes should read more than she was ready to acknowledge even to herself.   But whatever the reason of her strange feeling of happiness, she instinctively resumed her usual calm demeanor as she finished her toilet and went down to meet her guests in the dining-room.

The breakfast could hardly be called a gay one, for the wives and sisters of the American Tories who had been spirited away by Marion's men were naturally in great agitation still over the ultimate fate of the prisoners; and ransom, exchange, and the thousand and one chances of war were the sole topics of conversation, while Colonel Moncriffe endeavored to encourage the ladies by taking a more cheerful view of the situation than he really felt. War, grim war, was coming home to the Tories as it had been so long a cause of torment to the Whigs, and in more than one fair breast there may have been an unspoken wish that they had been more kind — less cruel — to their former neighbors when exulting in the result of the siege.

Later, when the sun had dried the dew, the party trooped out on the avenue which formed an approach to the mansion, and Tarleton found himself, as he had been manœuvring to do, near Geraldine, with the others beyond earshot. Roy's escape had been discussed at the breakfast-table, and with infinite tact Geraldine had displayed but passing interest in the event, with the result that, subtle as he was, Tarleton remained in doubt whether the news was a relief to her heart or merely a matter of no moment, since she had obtained his life at her request. He felt his passion for the lovely American gaining strength every moment, and he had little doubt that if he put forth his full power of fascination he could win this beauty, who tantalized him by her coldness while she drew him on by her gracious air of gratitude. She was a problem to be solved, and what man of Tarleton's temperament could withstand the desire to read the solution?

"Madam," he said, and never was voice more caressing and seductive than his when it pleased him to make it so, "I trust you will permit me to

tell you of the unbounded admiration which fills
my breast when I reflect upon your attitude of
last night. What a position, and how exquisitely
you filled it! Your kindly feeling toward that
misguided young man, your confidence and trust
in my honor which enabled you to ask his life, his
monstrous arrogance and insolence, and finally the
unspeakable grace with which you permitted me
to render you a service. No words can convey to
you my delight at this sudden and unexpected opportunity to read your heart ; that maiden heart,
which has thus become the object of adoration to
Banastre Tarleton, who here begs you to permit
him to continue his suit for your hand, and to be
now and always the humblest of your slaves."

"Sir," said Geraldine simply, but with much
dignity, "you do me great honor by this somewhat sudden avowal. I cannot deny that I have
been for some months aware of your suit, which
has the sanction of my father and of yours, but I
am hardly prepared for such passion on your part.
What do you know of me, — the real Geraldine
Moncriffe, — and how can I believe in the sincerity
of an affection which is the growth of a single
night ? "

" But what a night! so pregnant with varied
emotions. Nay, any one of them would be sufficient to fill me with enthusiasm. Why deny my
sincere homage to them all ? "

" Perhaps, sir, I desire time to be wooed before
I am won."

"NOW AND ALWAYS THE HUMBLEST OF YOUR SLAVES"

"By heavens you shall have it, empress of Tarleton's heart," he cried, actually carried out of himself by the delicious touch of archness in her tone; "give me but opportunity (and there is none like the present) to prove to you that my impetuosity is tempered by my discretion."

"And your boldness by timidity; at this pace, sir, you bid fair to defeat the boon I asked."

Tarleton bit his lip with a smothered exclamation. Could it be possible that this lovely, tantalizing American was laughing at him? For his life he could not tell. The situation was a novel one, and, to a man accustomed to easy conquests, of unprecedented interest. Before he had time to reply to this last sally, Halleck, who had approached them unperceived, stood bowing at Geraldine's elbow.

"Lady Dolly's horses wait, and she bids me tell you she desires to make her farewell."

"Truly," responded Geraldine, "Colonel Tarleton will excuse me while I attend my guest," and with a graceful courtesy she left them to return to the house.

"How progresses your suit?" whispered Halleck, as they watched the charming figure flit across the grass.

"'T is hard to say." Tarleton's tone was a mixture of satisfaction and chagrin. "She has greater wit and more beauty than I ever imagined, but ' _Château qui parle_ ' — you know the rest."

CHAPTER XI

THE MOTH RETURNS TO THE CANDLE

ALLASTAR MURRAY had concluded his evening
task of looking over the last English mail, and
after arranging the governor's letters and papers
ready to his hand whenever it might please His
Excellency to peruse them, he made ready to start
for a walk, during which he could reflect how soon
he might discreetly visit Dumblane again. For
Murray had now reached the stage of making
haste slowly, as the Latin saying has it. and so
far had found it profitable, although it must be
confessed that he did not enjoy it.

He had not proceeded very far down the street
which led to the Thunderbolt road (so called because it extended to the little settlement which
Governor Oglethorpe had named thus, because as
he quaintly remarked, "after the fall of a thunderbolt a spring then uprose, which still smells of the
bolt," and whose sulphur waters were of some
repute among the early settlers), when he saw,
slowly approaching him, a lady mounted on a fine
horse which he recognized as one belonging to Colonel Prevost, and following her a black servant,

also mounted.   As he came nearer, Lady Dolly
drew up her horse and greeted him.

"A good-day to you, sir; have you heard the
news?"

"What news?" asked Murray, not being minded
to relate Cupid's story, but wondering if this
could be what the dame referred to.   "I am out
in search of something to amuse me, having had a
most tiresome evening poring over official papers
and letters."

"Then you do not know of my capture and rescue?" said Lady Dolly, enjoying the novelty of
the situation, now that the fright was over; "or
how a band of outlaws attacked Colonel Moncriffe's plantation and secured all his guests by
binding them to chairs and otherwise, and were
about to execute their savage purposes (Heaven
save me!   I had already offered them every jewel
I possessed, fearing some sinister ending), when a
brave band of troopers rode down from the fort
just in the nick of time, and put the invaders to
flight, and speadily rescued us.   My word, but
Colonel Tarleton was in a pretty rage; he had a
hand-to-hand tussle with the leader himself."

"And pray who were this party?" asked Murray, as she paused for breath; "and whence did
they come?"

"They called themselves Rangers, or Marion's
men."

"I thought as much; the Swamp Fox is, as a
rule, too wary to be caught, but in this instance

our men must have taken some of them prisoners, did they not?"

"None but the leader, for, alas, the Rangers made good their escape with some eight or more of our friends set on the saddles before them. And do you know, the leader was such a fine handsome, personable fellow, that, between ourselves, I am only half sorry that he also contrived to escape, though I left Colonel Moncriffe in a towering rage because he could not trace the manner of it."

"The manner of it? was there any blood shed in the matter?"

"No, for which Heaven be thanked. You see Tarleton was greatly elated by the capture of — what was it they called him? oh, Telfair, — Captain Telfair, yes, that is it; and he had the prisoner safely bestowed in a strongly barred room, whence there is no exit except by the passage where the guards were placed; and, lo, this morning my gentle outlaw is found missing, and there are strong suspicions that, having sold himself to the devil for the sake of his freedom, he disappeared through the keyhole with a witch on a broomstick."

"Lady Dolly, you are incorrigibly fond of a jest," said Murray, unable to help laughing, as the merry dame pursued her tale with evident relish, and an air of mock mystery. "What do you mean me to conclude?"

"What you please, sir; half the whites and all the blacks on the plantation will vow he escaped by supernatural agency."

" 'T is much more probable by the assistance of some of the blacks aforesaid ; many of them are secretly on the side of the Whigs, and I confess myself skeptical as to the broomstick."

" That appears to me the most delightful stroke of all. But, stay, who comes yonder ? Is it — can it be Selwyn ? Now we shall hear the postscriptum of my story," and Lady Dolly trotted up the street, as the horseman was evidently going toward the fort. With brisk footsteps Murray followed her, and found that it was indeed Ensign Selwyn, looking somewhat soiled and travel-worn, but otherwise quite unhurt, and none the worse for his temporary imprisonment.

" What is that you tell me, Lady Dolly ? " he said, as Murray came within hearing. " Do I understand that Captain Telfair has indeed made his escape from Glenmoira ? "

" Certainly, the manner of his going is bewildering in its possibilities of the supernatural, but the fact remains that the gentleman is probably now journeying whence he came."

" I can find it in my heart to be devoutly thankful," said Selwyn, and then explained how he had been compelled to give his parole until due exchange could be made of prisoners, and that Colonel Marion was holding Sir Charles Adderly as hostage for the safety of his young officer. " I can tell you I did not spare my nag," he continued, looking down at his wet and tired animal, " for I am aware of Tarleton's reputation for the speedy stamping out of treason, and my mind misgave me sorely, as I counted poor Sir Charles' chances but small under the circumstances."

"And you were actually in the camp of those daring outlaws?" demanded Lady Dolly, still eager in the pursuit of knowledge as regarded every event in this strange and novel land and its inhabitants. "How did you fancy a close view of this terror of the province, this Marion? Is he a ruffian and of bloodthirsty propensities?"

Selwyn laughed. "Faith, it would add zest to the tale could I thus depict him. No, Lady Dolly, he is small and alert, with an air of great composure and command, and while he issued his orders to me it was with that courtly air which enforces respect. Indeed, it was only when addressing the American Tories that he spoke in anger, and I do assure you that I would hardly care to rest under the sting of such rebuke as he administered to them. But I must on to the fort and make my report to Colonel Prevost. May I have the honor to escort you, Lady Dolly? Do not forget, Murray, that you are supping with me this evening, and thank Marion, rebel though he be, that I am thus able to keep my appointment." But as he raised his hat in farewell to Lady Dolly, who thus pursued her way to the city, Murray also turned about and retraced his steps, wondering as he went whether it would be wise and prudent to advise the family at Dumblane of Roy Telfair's escape.

"No," he said to himself, "they will be likely to hear of it if from no other source than the blacks. How rejoiced Rose will be, and how full of quips and jests on the mystery! I'll warrant she rings the changes on British stupidity and Tory dullness, and I will not be able to catch her tripping or even making an admission as to the manner of his midnight flitting." From which reflections it will be seen that Murray was beginning to appreciate the ready wit and quick resource of his American sweetheart in a fashion which would have caused her the keenest enjoyment.

Just before sunset, as Murray started forth for his evening walk, in the forest that skirted Musgrove Swamp and not far from the direct road to Savannah, there drew up a covered cart, from which descended the short, squat figure of a man. He threw the reins on his horse's back, and after ransacking for a moment in the back part of the vehicle, produced a bag from whence he took a wooden measure of corn, and after setting it down on the ground by the horse, he returned to the cart.

"Wake up, Franz," he said, speaking in German, in a somewhat slow, but pleasant voice. "You must be rested by now, and it is best for us to take supper here, as I do not wish to reach the city too early."

"Yes, father," said Franz Hartzel, giving himself a shake, and rubbing his eyes as he jumped over the wheel to the ground; "shall we light a fire and make some coffee? Here are sticks in plenty, and dry ones, too."

"No, Franz. Did not thy mother bestow some home-brewed beer with the meat and bread? Ah, I thought so; beer is better than even the hot coffee for us Saltzburgers."

The boy and his father sat down on the grass beside the cart, after carefully surveying the spot lest it should be an abiding place for snakes, and were enjoying their supper with the spice of healthy appetites, when they became aware of a slight rustle in the undergrowth not far from them.

"Hist," said Hans Hartzel, "some one comes yonder; if it be those redcoat soldiers remember we are bringing the farm produce to the city for sale."

"I will not forget, father," answered the boy, quietly munching his bit of corn bread, with an air of unconcern. There was a moment's pause as both listened intently without appearing to do so, and then the figure of a man broke through the thicket and came toward them.

"Which way, friend?" asked Hans, rising and speaking in fairly good English. "Will you have a bite of bread and a bottle of mine own home-brewed beer?"

"Thank you for your hospitality," answered the new-comer. "I accept it heartily, for I forgot to take my breakfast, and having gone fasting all day find traveling on foot is hungry business."

Franz sprang up to find a fresh supply of food from the cart, and as he did so, Hans said in a low voice, with a good-humored smile: "Any and all of the Swamp Fox's men are welcome to share what I have, and if Captain Telfair does not remember me I have not forgotten him, nor the kindness he once did my hausfrau."

Roy started as the German laid his hand on his sleeve, and surveyed him closely. "I confess you had me at advantage. 'T is Hans Hartzel, from Ebenezer. I do remember the night I lay hid at your house, and helped the frau watch the sick boy; and if my small knowledge of medical treatment was of service you are most welcome to it. Is this the lad?"

"Yes, and a hearty, well-grown fellow for his years. How can I serve you, beside begging you to share our simple meal?"

"What brings you here?" asked Roy, to whom the beer tasted more delicious than any wine he had ever drunk. "Are you carrying garden stuff to the city?"

"Aye, the governor, yonder, deals with my frau, and thinks her eggs and chickens of the best. But," Hans looked cautiously over his shoulder, "wait; I'll send the boy out of earshot. Franz, go carefully to the road and watch there, lest any one surprise us."

Franz nodded, and ran rapidly away as his father turned back to continue his conversation. "Do you come from the Herr Colonel to-day?" he asked.

" I have but just escaped imprisonment by the British, and am on my way back to camp. Colonel Marion was to be in this vicinity for some days longer, before returning to South Carolina. My men made a capture of some importance, and but for bad fortune I should have been with them and carried back the prisoners."

" Then that was the party I met this morning, south of Ebenezer. I am engaged at present on a mission for the Herr Colonel."

" Indeed ; may I ask what, if it be not secret ? "

" Listen ; I would be glad of your counsel. Do you know one of the patriots in Savannah, named McAlpine ? "

" Oh, aye ; the hero of many hair-breadth escapades. What of him ? "

" I have a letter for him which must reach him without fail before to-morrow night, and I think, from what I gathered of the talk in camp, that there is a plan on foot which concerns surprising the fort." As he spoke there was a sudden rushing, crackling noise overhead, and Roy sprang to his feet just in time, for a great branch, which must long before have rotted and decayed, fell crashing to the ground. Poor Hans was not so lucky, for being older and stouter, he was in the act of rising when the branch struck him, and throwing him down, rendered him blind and senseless. Franz, hearing the noise, came running back, pale with terror.

" Quick, lad, help me to raise the branch off his

arm; there, turn him on his side and let me examine his injury," and Roy knelt down and after a few anxious moments succeeded in restoring Hans to consciousness. No bones seemed broken, but the shock had been great, and every time he attempted to move he turned so ill and faint that finally he lay back on the ground and declared his inability to proceed further. Franz stood gazing at his father with great dismay, and Roy suggested placing the injured man in the cart and taking him back to Ebenezer.

"Nay, nay; that will never do," said Hans, comprehending their intention; "what will become of my mission?"

"I'll do your errand," said Telfair quietly.

"But it would not be safe for you to reënter Savannah," interrupted Hans.

"Did you not say the message was urgent? Why consider my safety?"

"Aye; then listen; I have a plan. Leave me here, safely bestowed under yonder group of trees whose branches seem safe enough, and do you put on my gray blouse which is within the cart, and take Franz with you, for they know the lad in the city, and drive to the governor's mansion, deliver the eggs and vegetables, and then contrive to execute the other errand. You can safely pass for a neighbor of mine, Gottlieb Reiter, who is about your height and build and has darker hair than most of us; and if you could manage a few words of German" —

"I can readily do that," interposed Telfair, in that language.

"So!" ejaculated Hans, in pleased surprise, "then you are safe enough if you keep your face well concealed, or will use a little juice of the mulberry to darken your skin."

"But I hardly like to leave you here," said Roy, after hearing a few more instructions from Hans, "and surely I can take the cart and return without Franz, who I think should stop with you here."

"For what? a few bruises and a sick stomach? No, take the lad; he may prove more useful than you think."

"But stop, Hans; it strikes me that I can arrange the plan better. If I drive now to the governor's I will be very apt to encounter just those whom I wish to avoid, for at this hour after supper, it is the custom for the gentlemen and their friends to take air in the gardens, and while you might escape critical examination, it would be just my fortune to experience it. I know the usual haunts of McAlpine, and I also know a place where I can put up the cart and horse for the night. I will go there first, leaving Franz here with you. He can join me at an early hour in the morning, near the store by the tall chimney which still stands in the burned quarter. If I am not there by seven o'clock, then proceed to Tondee's tavern at the corner of Broughton and Whitaker streets."

"Very good; here, find the letter," and he indicated where it was concealed on his person. " Franz, turn the horse; 't is a good beast, and can travel well, even better under the saddle than with my cart. Now stain your face a bit, not forgetting your hands; I fear the blouse is over wide for you."

" Not so wide," said Telfair, as he drew it together across his broad shoulders, " but a trifle short; however, one hardly expects elegance of attire when arrayed in a blouse shirt. Now for the mulberry juice; I saw plenty of them on the other side of the road," and he plunged through the thicket in that direction. When he returned a short time after, his disguise was fairly good, and after receiving due admonition as to the proper price to be paid for the contents of the cart, Roy finally mounted the seat, Franz having led the horse back to the road, and waving a good-by, he drove away.

The sun had set, and the shadows were lengthening as the covered cart made its way into the city. The driver sat slouching forward in the seat, and the horse ambled along in a leisurely fashion, which by no means suggested the speed the animal was capable of. After picking the way carefully along, Roy turned into South Broad Street, then almost a country road, with a few scattered houses all on the north side, the chiefest of these being a public (as the inn was called), owned by Eppinger, at the northeast corner of Jefferson Street. Here were several men, lounging and drinking, and as Roy drew his cart up in front of the door, one of them called out: —

"Here comes a country man well laden; go, boy, and see if the larder needs replenishing."

A black fellow of about eighteen ran out, and Roy accosted him in broken English with an occasional German word.

"Lodging here for horse and man? I vonts feed for mine guten horse. He vas come thirty miles since sun-up."

"Yes, marse, plenty place under shed; I'll fotch him 'roun'."

But Roy did not seem willing to descend from his perch, so he drove around to the back of the house, following the black boy, who ran ahead, his object in so doing being to inspect the inmates of the room, whose windows he passed as he went. But the face he was looking for was not there, and it occurred to Roy that although the cart and horse might find shelter here, he would himself be safer elsewhere, for half the men lounging inside were soldiers from the fort, and he was not particularly anxious to cultivate their observation after his so recent encounter with some of their comrades. So he hesitated, and chaffered, and bargained, and finally pretending that he had a friend to see, turned the cart around, and again proceeded on his way.

It was now quite dark, save for the light of a young moon which drifted out of the clouds at intervals, and Roy drove along the streets, which in good colony times had been so neatly kept, but which now bore evidence, in many places, of the siege. He passed the house of Colonel McAlpine and drew the rein, then slacked it, as he reflected that Tondee's Tavern, on Broughton Street, was much more likely to harbor that gentleman's dare-devil relative, Roderick, who was as famous for his cups as his courage. And so proceeding, he drove through State Street, passing St. James Square, where the stately mansion occupied by Governor Wright stood, almost alone, surrounded by large, and for that period, well-kept garden and grounds. But if Roy was minded to pass the gate, not so his steed, for suddenly, without any warning of his intention, that animal stopped short, and Roy, who happened to be leaning forward, was shot out of his seat and over the shafts to the ground, striking his head as he went against the gatepost. And having accomplished as much harm as possible, the horse gave forth a plaintive, long-drawn whinny, and stood still.

Roy was not stunned, though he ought to have been, by the shock, but he lay still, seeing stars and feeling giddy for several minutes, until roused by the sound of an imperious voice demanding who was blocking the way, and another which said laugh-ingly, —

"Some country yokel has evidently left his horse and cart standing outside while he makes love to the maidservants; did you harm yourself as you ran against the wheel?"

"Not I; the blow has merely detached my fob from my watch. Stand still a moment, Murray, I think I can fasten it," and Halleck steadied himself against the cart-wheel as he spoke. "Selwyn's port was somewhat heady; I'll take some coffee with you, and then to bed, as I slept none last night."

Roy lay still; they had not perceived him, as he was hidden by the other wheel of the cart. The horse, having done his worst, seemed disposed to be quiet, and bent down his head, munching a stray tuft of grass which had sprung up outside the gate.

"To resume," said Halleck, going back to what had evidently been the topic of their conversation as they approached, "you cannot think how monstrous amusing the whole affair is to me. I have seen Tarleton through half an hundred romantic and mad fancies, but nothing has ever approached in intensity his passion for the fair Moncriffe. By gad, sir, his face when she flouted him this morning was a study that even a friend might smile over," and his laugh rang out at the recollection. "Why, man, Tarleton the irresistible, Tarleton the indifferent, the cynical, was left standing there agape, while she walked off tranquilly. And I never saw him so nonplussed in my life. '*Château qui parle*,' he said to me. What will you take as to the chances, Murray, of his success?"

"Nothing; she may be dazzled by his position or even bewitched by the conquest of one so well-known as a breaker of hearts. 'T is hard to tell a woman's way."

"Ay; and there is, I am told, the complication of a former swain."

"Indeed!" said Murray in a tone of surprise. "Do you speak by the card?"

"So far as that Mistress Molly Durbeville confided to me that there had been rumors of love passages between our lovely hostess and a Whig gentleman, whose name she would not divulge — I think because she feared I might tell Tarleton and bring vengeance on some rebel's head (for Mistress Molly has leanings that way, I fancy). Tarleton has sworn to win the fair Geraldine, and he would move even hell itself, were that possible, to gain the object of a passion which, though it may be short-lived, has the elements of a whirlwind while it abides. I love him much, as man to man, but with the gentle sex his way is to win, wear, and soon forsake. Come, Murray, my fob is mended; let 's on to the house and take a cup of Sir James's coffee before retiring."

Roy lay still until the echo of their footsteps died away. Then he sprang up, his eyes alight, his heart beating wildly.

"Have I been mad to doubt her?" he thought. "Oh, Geraldine, my darling, while the faintest ray of hope lights my breast, not man nor devil shall tear us asunder!"

CHAPTER XII

"SHE WOULD AND SHE WOULDN'T"

TONDEE'S TAVERN on Broughton Street had been the well-known rendezvous for the patriots ever since the organizing of the Georgia Sons of Liberty and the Council of Safety when the war of independence began, and consequently it was a house always under surveillance after the British occupation in 1779. But try as those in authority did to maintain efficient police system, the patriots continued to evade it, and through the guests who most frequented that hostelry Marion received much of the secret information which enabled him to plan and make his raids upon the enemy with that rapidity and unerring certainty which made his name at once a terror and a success in the provinces of Georgia and South Carolina.

The day was yet young when a barefooted black boy came sleepily through the door of the tavern aforesaid, carrying a bucket of water which he proceeded to splash up and down the wooden floor of the front portico, preparatory to mopping the same. He had succeeded in wetting it pretty thoroughly when his attention was directed from the task he was lazily accomplishing by a shout from the room whose low window opened upon the portico.

"I say, boy, stop that infernal splashing long enough to tell some one to fetch me a morning punch. The sound of that water trickling down makes me thirsty. Egad, 't is the first time water ever affected me in any manner whatever," and the speaker thrust his head out of the window, laughing good-humoredly as he spoke.

"Laws, marse, dey ain't nobody 'round jes' yit," said the boy, setting down his bucket, "but ef yo' hole on fer a minute tel I git dis yere done, I 'll come an' help yo' fin' de bottles."

"Oh, if it 's a matter of finding bottles, I can mix it myself," said the other, drawing back from the window, and proceeding to institute a search in the cupboard behind the low shelf which served as the bar. "I wonder what became of those two spies who were lounging here when I went to sleep; faith, I fancy I tired them out with my stories of Scotch wars." This remark was delivered in an undertone to himself, as he brought out tumbler and bottles. At last, finding what he sought, he poured it into the glass, and was about drinking the mixture when he became aware that a head (not belonging to the black boy) was thrust inside the window, and its owner was quietly regarding him.

Roderick McAlpine drank long and deep, regardless of the stranger's scrutiny, and then setting down the empty glass, turned toward the window.

" Good-day, sir," said Roy Telfair politely ; " if you will invite me I will join in your morning refreshment, providing you do not object to my vaulting over the window-sill, as the doorway is flooded with water."

"On my word, sir, you have easy manners," returned McAlpine, as Roy sprang in and approached him ; "not that I am lacking in hospitality, but " —

" You prefer to select the object of it," interrupted Roy, making the secret sign which was used by the Rangers. " Pardon my early intrusion, but I searched the house for you last night, met with a misadventure which detained me, and spent the night in a cart full of farm produce, which I have left, with the horse tied carefully to a tree, just around the corner there, feeling sure that I could get some news of you here."

" But I know you, sir," said the other, surveying him keenly as his dark eyes scrutinized the disguise of the supposed countryman ; " and you wore a lighter skin and coat of another color under the trees in the Swamp Fox's camp. Captain Telfair, what can I do for you ? "

" I bring you this letter; it was first intrusted to other hands than mine ; give me word of mouth in return, as, after my business be ended in the city, I go direct to join Colonel Marion."

But McAlpine was engaged in deciphering the scrap of paper and paid no heed for a few seconds. Then he raised his head, looked round the room cautiously, and spoke in a whisper.

" 'T is a plan well arranged and matured, by which we hope to capture the fort, but it will take more forces than I conceive Colonel Marion can bring to aid at the present time. We have suborned several of the garrison, and are warned from Charleston of a spy, who travels with Tarleton's escort, and goes by the name of Norman Burt."

" Ay, a tall trooper; I know him, and I think he had a hand in my escape from Tarleton's band two days ago, when I stood good chance to be shot."

" Burt is one of the moving spirits in the affair. I have here a paper," and he drew it from an inside pocket, " which contains a plan, rudely done as you see, of the fort, and the places indicated where we may make entry provided we can surprise the garrison. Take this, and the rest shall go by word of mouth, but not till nightfall, as I must gather some information to-day which is of importance. Can you meet me between ten and eleven to-night in the peach orchard, behind the governor's mansion? He holds fête to-night, I am told, for the new beauty, Mistress Geraldine Moncriffe, and I shall mingle with the guests, as those I wish to see will be there."

A hot flush dyed Telfair's face. Was this then his opportunity to see Geraldine, and perhaps gain speech of her? The daring thought suited his impetuous temper, and he eagerly assured McAlpine that he would keep the appointment at the hour named, and hiding the paper containing the plan of Fort Wayne in his breast, he bade him farewell, and springing out of the window proceeded to find the horse and cart, which had remained apparently undisturbed in his absence.

The fête which Sir James Wright, governor of the province of Georgia, was about to give had been the subject of much talk and gossip, as it would serve the double purpose of celebrating the return of British rule and of compliment to the daughter of the officer who had taken prominent part in the siege, and with the exception of the few houses still occupied by the Whigs who dared to remain in the city, there was not a resident who had not been included in the invitations, and consequently Savannah felt in a properly gala mood. Flags floated on the fort and the governor's mansion, and the sun rose brightly over the waters of the bay. It was rumored that a gay party was expected from Charleston, who were coming by sloop, and this added to the interest of the affair, as even in those early days there was generous social rivalry between the two cities.

Molly Durbeville, sitting in her window on Broughton Street, watched the carts and pedestrians as they passed, most of them, as she shrewdly conjectured, on the way to the scene of the night's festivities, and she commented on each in her usual lively fashion: "There goes the third black boy carrying vines, Anne; I am sure they must be decking the whole pavilion, which is to be set in the garden. And here are flags; oh, ay, no doubt for the ballroom, — and one, two, four carts, filled with provisions. See this covered one. I am sure that is from Ebenezer; yes, there's the same bright-looking lad whom I purchased the roots and vines from last year, which reminds me that I need a few more to replenish those that have not flourished. Here, lad, here," calling and waving her hand, "stop a moment;" and greatly to the horror of her more decorous sister, Molly flew out of the door and ran down to the cart.

Franz, who was driving, drew up his horse obediently, as Molly accosted him. "Do you remember me? I had vines of you last year."

"Yes," said Franz, nodding back at the pleasant-voiced maid, "did the lady want more? I have not them to-day; I go to take mine load to the governor's."

"I thought so, but just let me look " — and then Molly stopped abruptly, for back in the cart she saw a pair of eyes that even beneath the battered hat she recognized, and the bright color deserted her face with rapidity born of consternation. Telfair smiled, and laid a finger on his lips, but Molly impulsively ran around the cart and whispered to him, —

"How dare you be here! for Heaven's sake take care, and seek better disguise."

"I am on the way to secure such," he answered; "keep my counsel and receive my thanks."

Molly returned to the house much more soberly

than she left it, and watched the cart out of sight
as it drove slowly around the corner of Jefferson
Street and disappeared, but she pondered much
and long that day, and did not recover her spirits
until she commenced to dress for the fête.

Sir James Wright's guests began to arrive be-
times for the governor's fête, which comprised, first,
a stately ceremonial in the way of a reception held
in the pavilion erected a short distance from the
mansion. Next, the dance, which was arranged in
the house, a whole floor having been cleared for
the purpose; and lastly, the abundant supper, that
was served at half past ten o'clock and continued,
together with the dancing, until broad daylight, if
it suited the guests to remain until the sun rose.

The pavilion was lighted with wax lights and
hung with wreaths of green and flowers, and the
path to and from it to the mansion lighted by lan-
terns fixed to the trees, which cast a light sufficient
to penetrate a short distance into the garden, beyond which lay the peach orchard that ran back to
South Broad Street and there straggled off in a
westerly direction. As a chronicler of the times
quaintly remarks, the fête " was the most numer-
ous and brilliant appearance ever known in the
town, and was long talked of and discussed in the
social circles of Savannah."

When Geraldine, accompanied by her father and
Colonel Tarleton, entered the pavilion a soft murmur of admiration ran around the room, for even
her stately court gown did not detract from her

beauty and grace; and the touch of powder on her hair brought out the rose-leaf tint of her complexion, while the diamonds that glittered on her neck seemed to reflect the sparkle of her blue eyes. Tarleton, chapeau in hand, approached Lady Dolly, who, dressed in a marvelous "atlas gown of blue and gold with flowered petticoat" (again we quote the chronicler), was doing the honors of the evening, with her merry yet courtly air, and bade Geraldine stand beside her until it should please His Excellency to open the ball with her.

Geraldine, it must be said, was in the highest possible spirits. All day long she had teased and tormented Tarleton, never once allowing him to pass the barrier she had so coquettishly laid down, and even evading her father's evident desire to obtain some definite assurance of her satisfaction with the proposed alliance. But why her heart bounded so lightly within her bosom Geraldine would not acknowledge, albeit she could not restrain a smile when Margot, having completed her careful toilet, said gravely, as she surveyed her with bland satisfaction, —

"Ah, my leddy, the air o' the plantation has done mickle for ye since yester e'en; I wadna think ye the same lassie that fell asleep wi' tears in her bonnie blue e'."

But Geraldine only shook her head playfully as she went down the gallery. Not even to Margot would she confess that the magic which had changed her mood was the timely escape of a rebel and an ingrate.

Outside the mansion about the time of Geraldine's arrival, down in the peach orchard, beside a horse which he had tied to one of the trees, stood Roy Telfair. He had changed his dress for that of a seafaring man, and restored his face to its usual complexion, depending upon a wide hat low over his brow, and a blue handkerchief around his neck for concealment, as he argued that he would probably have to run for it should his way be challenged, and in the haste of his departure, aided by the uncertain light, could escape recognition. Capture with the plan of the fort upon him meant a spy's death; but even so, he would dare all for his country's sake.

He waited with what patience he could, creeping about in the shadow of the trees, for McAlpine, and at last was relieved by seeing him saunter carelessly into the summer-house. A low call of the whippoorwill made it certain, and skirting along the side of the house he met McAlpine at the door.

"I have seen four of the men I hoped to find," said McAlpine in low tones, stepping back in the shade made by the vines, "and you may say to Marion for me that the raid cannot take place before the change of the moon. I have still one more patriot to hold counsel with, but slipped away lest you should deem me unable to keep the rendezvous; if so be you can tarry without suspicion for a half hour longer I will return, but further from this point — Hist! I hear voices. Wait if you can; if not speed on at the expiration of the half hour, and by all means protect yourself." Roy glided back to the place where his horse stood tied, and McAlpine, humming a Scotch air, went carelessly back toward the pavilion.

"Mistress Moncriffe, I solicit the honor of your hand in the opening contra-dance," said Sir James some half hour later, bowing profoundly; and then led the way through the garden to the ballroom, where the band from the fort sent forth inspiring music as the gay company entered and formed for the dance named, Lady Dolly and Tarleton leading from the other end. Slow and stately was the movement (in contrast to ours of a later day), and many the admiring glances cast on the principal performers by those who looked on, awaiting their turn as etiquette demanded.

After the formal opening the dancing became general, and Geraldine's partners were so many that Tarleton, to his chagrin, was only able to obtain a fourth or fifth dance from the pretty Tory. But with his usual adroitness, he sought out those guests whom he had met at Glenmoira, dancing in turn with them while consumed with inward impatience for his return to Geraldine.

Allastar Murray, having been so fortunate as to secure one of the coveted dances, enjoyed it even beyond his expectation, for a casual mention of Dumblane gave Geraldine her opportunity, and all unconscious that she was delighting her listener, she poured forth her love and admiration for Rose into his delighted ears, and thereby secured to herself a loyal and faithful admirer. And being loath to leave so interesting a topic at the end of the dance, Murray proposed a stroll in the garden, and Geraldine, feeling the heat of the ballroom, gladly acquiesced, and they walked quietly and unperceived forth into the night.

"Oh, how lovely!" said Geraldine as they followed the path that led beyond the pavilion toward the orchard, where the trees were making exquisite shadows in the growing moonlight. "I think Sir James said there were seats in the pleasaunce, — yes, there are some, beneath that vine."

"Better still, the summer-house; I fear the dew is falling and you are not yet acclimated. This Southern air, soft though it be, is very different from our Scotch breezes."

"True, I had forgotten; then we will try the summer-house." But as she spoke a strange, swift shiver crept over Geraldine and with a light laugh she said, "You are wise to warn me; I think perhaps we had best return, cool and grateful though the air is, for I am somewhat chilly here now, unless you will fetch me my scarf which I carelessly left somewhere in the pavilion. Thank you," as Murray acquiesced; "no, I will await you here; it can do me no harm, for I will pin my kerchief across my breast."

Murray sped away, and Geraldine, seating her-

self on the wooden bench, gave a low sigh as she
enjoyed the luxury of being alone and off her
guard for a few brief moments.   And so, of course,
fate took instant advantage, for, intent upon her
thoughts, she never heard a footstep brush the
grass and steal across the threshold, till with a wild
start she came back from her dreams, to feel a
strong arm around her and hear a tender voice say
in the tone she had never forgotten, "Geraldine,
my own, forgive me, and believe that I was mad to
doubt you."

For a brief instant she lay still in his embrace,
half terrified at the wave of emotion that swept
over her, then she tore herself away.

"Roy, Roy, is it really you?   Oh, how can you
tempt death and destruction thus?   I have been
so happy in the belief that you" — she paused
with trembling lips, which he, half beside himself
at her change of mood, bent down and kissed.
"Oh, you are not safe here for one brief moment.
Go, go, I do beseech you."

"Not till I hear that you forgive — that you
love me still, that this hateful alliance will never
be consummated," and he threw himself on his knees
before her.

"Alas, I cannot tell," she sighed softly; "what
is a dutiful daughter to decide when her father
commands?"

"Consult your own heart and answer me here
and now.   That you did love me I truly believe;
that you still love me I hope as for my salvation."

" I stand I hardly know how between two fires, either of which threatens to destroy me."

" Nay, sweetheart, if you view me with terror that is a deathblow to love. Kiss me once and say farewell."

" Ah," a little, fond heart-breaking cry. " Oh, for some guide to show me the way out of this labyrinth ! "

" Geraldine, let your heart speak ; dismiss these dreams of ambition and be true to your noblest self. Bend your lovely eyes to mine, love ; in their blue depths I can see that almost against your will you are loyal to your country and to me."

" I had better close my eyes since they are such telltales and say so much," she whispered with a low laugh, and then as she uttered the arch confession, looking behind them toward the pavilion, to her horror she saw approaching in the moonlight the figure not of Murray, but Tarleton. Oh, kind Heaven, could she rescue Roy again, and how ?

" Rise, sir," she said, in a voice so cold and scornful that Roy gazed at her in stunned surprise, unable to account for her sudden change of manner, " rise and annoy me no more. I am indeed amazed at your presumption and must ask that you leave me instantly."

" Mistress Moncriffe has here a protector and defender," cried Tarleton, darting to her side, as Telfair, scarce able to believe his ears, staggered to his feet. " Well, sir," as he suddenly recognized his former prisoner, " you are a braver man even than I thought, since not content with again putting your head in the lion's mouth you dare to aspire to the lady whom Tarleton claims "—

" By God, sir, your claims shall be promptly settled," cried Roy, pale with fury, and as Murray came suddenly upon the group, he saw him strike Tarleton lightly upon the face with the palm of his hand. " I am ready to give all the satisfaction you demand, and more. Murray, your sword will answer my purpose," and, snatching the rapier which Murray wore at his side, Roy cried, " On guard, sir," as he made a pass at Tarleton and drove him across the threshold of the summerhouse to the grass beyond.

Tarleton's sword flew from its sheath, his eyes blazing, even as he debated whether he should call for aid to secure his former prisoner, but the presence of Geraldine forbade the treachery, and besides it would be easy enough to secure Telfair after he (one of the best swordsmen in the British army) had disarmed him and taught this saucy rebel a much needed lesson. For a few seconds nothing was heard except the clash of steel and the hurried breathing of the combatants; then Telfair began to push his adversary with surprisingly swift strokes, and suddenly, with a wonderful quickness which the lookers-on hardly realized, there was a flash, a gleam of bright steel in the moonlight, as Tarleton's sword flew from his hand and he stood absolutely at Telfair's mercy.

" So turns the wheel of fortune," said Telfair,

as he calmly possessed himself of the weapon.
" Yours yesterday, mine to-day.   I give you your
life, sir, as you gave me mine ; accept the gift at
the hands of a rebel whom you scorned, but who
has at least taught you that he is worthy of respect.
I regret that an engagement with Colonel Marion
compels me to leave you somewhat abruptly.   Take
your sword," and he flung it contemptuously at
Tarleton's feet, " I will not burden myself with so
bloody a weapon ; but remember when next you
meet an American on the field that one of them
gave you the quarter you denied his countrymen,"
and before his passionate, ringing tones had fairly
died on the air, he thrust his sword into Murray's
hand and plunged among the shadows of the trees.

For an instant the group stood as if paralyzed,
but choking though he was with mortification and
rage, Tarleton was the first to recover himself.
" Help, help," he shouted, as he dashed up the
path and ran full against Selwyn and McAlpine,
" to horse with all speed ; that ubiquitous rebel,
Telfair, has just escaped through the orchard, and
unless he be the devil himself we can stop him
this time."

Selwyn dropped McAlpine's arm and joined
Tarleton in the hue and cry, the result of which
was that several officers and men, with Tarleton at
their head, were soon mounted and in hot pursuit
up Jefferson Street, where they debated for a moment which way to proceed.

Geraldine, clinging to Murray's arm, felt a

deadly faintness creep over her, although she struggled for composure.

"You cannot walk," cried Murray, "let me fly for a glass of wine; rest here. Oh, sir," to McAlpine, who approached them on his way to see if aught had befallen Telfair, "assist Mistress Moncriffe for an instant until I return."

"It is hardly necessary," faltered Geraldine, sinking on the bench of the summer-house as Murray ran hastily toward the pavilion. "You are most kind, sir. Do you think — is it possible — that Captain Telfair can escape?" There was such a note of agony in her voice that McAlpine, who had been about to make a far different assurance, said kindly, —

"Why not? Marion and his men bear charmed lives, they say, and Telfair has doubtless provided for his own security. Hark! we cannot hear distinctly, but I am sure that a horseman is racing out on South Broad Street; trust him to double on his pursuers."

It was indeed Roy, as McAlpine shrewdly surmised, and he had a few precious minutes' start, as he had calculated. But as he turned again to take the road that led out by Musgrove Swamp he heard the rapid beat of horses' hoofs and knew they were hot upon his trail. Hans' horse was proving himself a gallant beast, and he headed him straight for the water, pulling out his pistol as he rode and thrusting the telltale plan of the fort inside it as a wad, determined that he would save it if he could, or thus destroy it if forced to shoot. On, on, but the hoof-beats were coming nearer; one more desperate effort, and the bend in the road touched the shore, where he could leave the horse and hide in the swamp.

The tide was coming in over the swamp, and springing from his horse, Telfair flung the reins over the good beast's neck, and plunged deep into the water. As he did so, he could both hear and see the group of mounted men who paused bewildered to survey the tired horse, but a faint sound at his left, where grew a cluster of low trees which would afford him concealment, made him turn his head. The bushes parted, and as he swam nearer he saw, in their shadow, an Indian canoe, and in the boat, regarding him silently, sat Ossaba. A moment longer and Roy clambered over its side, and sank breathless and in safety on the bottom of the boat, as the bushes closed over their heads.

CHAPTER XIII

LADY DOLLY ACCEPTS THE RÔLE OF CONFIDANTE

"My cup of chocolate at once; I have actually waited ten minutes, and I must make my toilet by twelve."

"Yes, madam, it is not my fault that your orders are not fulfilled. These African servants are both slow and lazy and have apparently no account of time," replied Lady Dolly's prim English maid. "If your ladyship would be pleased to speak "—

"But I'm not pleased about anything," retorted Lady Dolly sleepily, from between the bed curtains. "I am half dead from dancing until four o'clock this morning, and really, Simpson, as that chocolate is so tardy, you may fill me a glass of liqueur from the cabinet yonder;" and her ladyship yawned and thrust one pretty bare foot outside the coverlet as she spoke. Simpson fetched the liqueur as she was bid, and presently came a rap on the chamber door, and a salver made its appearance containing a pot of steaming chocolate, accompanied by hot corn-bread which Lady Dolly managed to swallow with keen relish, talking the while busily to her maid.

"It was the prettiest fête I've seen since I left

home," declared she, draining her second cup of chocolate with unabated appetite. "There is a species of novelty about the social element, and with due ceremony at one moment, a curious lack of it the next, which appeals to me. I trust you had some refreshments, Simpson, for I believe I kept you waiting an unconscionable time."

"Yes, my lady, we were all served after coming in from the garden, where we servants ran when the hue and cry sounded, and I was like to die of fright because the blacks declared that it was a raid of Marion's men, and I expected nothing but that we should all be taken prisoners."

"And carried off to mountain fastnesses," cried Lady Dolly, laughing in high glee. "Oh, Simpson, what an opportunity was lost! If those bold outlaws only had appeared — think what an adventure to have told when we return home!"

"Yes, madam," replied Simpson meekly, but inwardly giving thanks that her madcap mistress was safely bestowed in bed, instead of under the greenwood tree she aspired to; "will you have the blue or the purple paduasoy this morning?"

"Oh, the blue, by all means; 't is a delicate compliment to the brave young fellow who so successfully made his escape. On my word," and Lady Dolly sighed softly with an air of sentiment as she rose, "if I stop here among these extraordinary people longer, I shall awake some morning and find myself a rebel of the deepest — I mean bluest — dye."

"I thought, your ladyship, that the color adopted by these outlaws was green. I 'm sure that is what they wore that awful night on the plantation."

"Oh, ay ; blue in New York, green in Georgia, but all of them tarred with the same stick," said Lady Dolly, laughing. "I really am anxious about that reckless young man. Fancy his daring to challenge Colonel Tarleton when he might be surrounded and captured at any moment. Did you hear whether he made his escape by land or water?" It must be confessed that Lady Dolly loved to gossip, whether it be with her maid up-stairs, or in the drawing-room below, and Simpson was perfectly aware of the fact, so she retailed a highly colored and picturesque account of Captain Telfair's adventures, with an added detail to the effect that some supernatural agency certainly superintended his fortunes, or his capture would have been inevitable.

"Pooh!" said Lady Dolly as she arrayed herself in the blue paduasoy, which was most becoming to her blonde coloring, "if I had the cross-examining of those blacks on the plantation I 'll wager I 'd have got to the bottom of that mystery. What 's that at my door, Simpson? Some one knocks."

In response to the summons, Simpson presently informed her mistress that Colonel Tarleton was below and craved the pleasure of seeing her, which information caused a slight flutter on the part of that fair lady, who, nevertheless, contrived

to descend in another ten minutes, filled with over-
powering curiosity and no little mischief.

The drawing-room of Colonel Prevost's residence was a long, low-ceilinged room, with windows
looking out on the bay, and in one of them stood
Tarleton, with somewhat frowning brow, as Lady
Dolly entered.

"A good day to you, sir. You are early astir
after the festivities of last night, or rather this
morning," giving him her hand, upon which he
instantly pressed a kiss, "and you look as fresh as
if you had not been doing duty both as carpet-
knight and soldier. By the bye, how far out did
your pursuit of that lively and ubiquitous young
man take you?"

"Just a mile up the road, where we found an
old and rather blown nag standing riderless (it
was claimed by a Dutch lad, who told a pitiful tale
of how the rebel had stolen it from his cart where
the animal stood hitched on State Street), and for
the moment we were quite at fault; but the
troopers declared that our quarry had taken to the
swamp, and by the time we had finished debating
the point, we were forced to abandon it for lack of
boat to explore, though they tell me that Musgrove Swamp is a devilish good place for both
hiding and drowning."

Lady Dolly gave way to laughter. and after
frowning for a moment, Tarleton joined her.
"Forgive me," she said, taking breath again, "the
humorous side is uppermost in me to-day."

"'He laughs best who laughs last,'" quoted Tarleton somewhat grimly, but aware that he could not wholly conceal his discomfiture and rage from the quick-witted lady, although he prayed devoutly that she had not yet heard the disastrous end of his duel with Telfair. "But a truce to this episode, which I own causes me chagrin. I came to see you for a far different cause."

"Indeed," regarding him intently; "then 't is love, not war, that makes your errand."

He smiled at her readiness as he made answer: "Ay, and 'pon honor, for the first time I am minded to ask one of your sex about another."

"Ah, Tarleton, to what a pass do I see you brought — gay gallant as you are — by this fair and subtle American!"

"You are right," he cried, with such infinite passion and earnestness that Lady Dolly was startled into gravity. "I half believe I am bewitched, for her beauty entrances me while her coldness maddens me. You are wise — tell me, shall I press her for definite assurance that I may win her, or give her what she asks of me — time?"

"Has it then gone so far? Women, like horses, love to have their heads given them, and I do think whip and spur a mistake, under most circumstances, with either!"

"You may be right." He sighed, walked back and forward a few restless steps, and then resumed: "That fellow," with concentrated hatred in his tone that made Lady Dolly open wide her eyes and stare at him, — "that fellow has the audacity to admire her; damn him!"

"Fie, fie," shaking her head in pretended horror at the oath; "what do you mean? Not the gentleman who does the disappearing act so cleverly?"

"Ay, I found him on his knees before her in the summer-house."

"Oh!" said Lady Dolly to herself; and it was a very large round O, and meant at least a quarto volume of comprehension. But aloud she murmured softly, "What presumption! I trust Mistress Moncriffe reproved him promptly?"

"Faith, she did, and almost summoned me to her side by her answer. And I rushed to her," — Tarleton caught himself just in time.

"And he escaped," cried Lady Dolly, now fully convinced that in the encounter between the two men, Tarleton had been worsted, and unable to help a little private exultation over the dashing rebel whom in her naughty heart she admired. "Why, man, the field is open for you, but for Heaven's sake ride carefully or you will be thrown."

Tarleton smiled at the racing simile. Sir Donald Menteith was master of hounds at home, and Lady Dolly dearly loved to follow the pack, and seldom failed to be in at the death.

"Then you counsel me to moderation? But war waits not for love, and I must soon leave this place to stamp out this rebellion against His Majesty. And you know I am somewhat given to impetuosity."

"I am aware 't is your most glaring fault," said Lady Dolly, with an amused recollection of certain passages between her and Tarleton before she changed her name and took Sir Donald for better or worse; "but let desire wait on expediency; believe me, 't is the wiser plan to-day. And now I must dismiss you, for I am going for a ride at noon and am sure to be late as it is. Farewell," and she courtesied to him with a merry smile.

Geraldine, unlike Lady Dolly, had made an early awakening, if indeed she could be said to have slept, for after conquering her faintness she had returned to the ballroom with Murray and danced every dance as she had promised, Tarleton returning in time to claim two of these, and so fearful was she of giving cause for gossip, or of allowing Tarleton for one moment to suppose that Telfair occupied her thoughts, that she unbent a little from her proud dignity and was almost restless in her gayety. Perhaps that added to her charm, for when she left the ballroom, even the feminine verdict of Savannah was in her favor.

It had been Geraldine's plan to stop that day in the city, but her father sent word by Margot that he should be detained at the fort on official business, and she therefore excused herself to her host, Sir James, and ordered her chariot to take her back to the plantation. But when it came around to the door, there came also Jumbo leading her own bay horse, and Geraldine promptly decided that Margot should return in the chariot, while she would ride with Jumbo as escort. And so bidding graceful farewells and thanks to the governor, she mounted and rode swiftly away, before Lady Dolly had finished her first cup of chocolate.

She had not gone far, however, on her homeward way, before she was seized with a curious, half-homesick longing to once more see Dumblane and her friend Rose. To be sure, her father was not friendly now with the Telfairs, but then he had made no remark when she told him of Rose's visit, nor had he forbidden her to return it. Why not? They were companions almost since babyhood; how could she be blamed for wanting to continue the bond of friendship even if this unholy war had intervened? So with a quiet word to Jumbo, who galloped back to deliver her message of where she was going to Margot, and to bid her go on to Glenmoira, Geraldine turned aside as she came to the cross-road, and cantered on up the avenue to Dumblane.

Rose, sitting with her mother on the portico, engaged in the homely and necessary employment of rolling bandages, which were to be sent, when opportunity afforded, to the forces of the patriots in South Carolina, could hardly believe her eyes when she saw the bay horse and beheld Geraldine waving a pretty salute to them, and she flew to meet her as she drew rein at the door.

"Welcome, thrice welcome," she cried, throwing her arms around her friend, forgetting in her warm-hearted affection the terms upon which they had parted, while Geraldine totally ignored the fact of her Tory sentiments, and embraced her rebel Rose with the utmost fervor. "Look, mother, is she not more lovely than ever? and grown, yes, though even now you are not so tall as I," and Rose gave a mock condescending glance at the red-gold head.

"I see but little change," said Madam Telfair, as she kissed the pretty cheek which glowed afresh under gaze of eyes so like those which had looked into her own a few hours before. "Yes," smiling, as she noted the girl's brief embarrassment, "you have the air of the world you lacked before, and I think have gained in self-control. I wish I could say as much for Rose, who, as you see, remains outspoken as ever."

"Who wants me otherwise must ride away," returned Rose gayly.

"I, for one, do not, although you did read me a lecture the other day," said Geraldine, with a teasing gleam in her eye; "but I came for only a brief moment, as I am returning home after the fête of last night."

"Oh, ay, the fête given by Sir James. I know you were the admired of all," said Rose in a voice of such hearty conviction that both her mother and Geraldine could not refrain from laughing.

"Not precisely all, Rose; indeed, if my memory serves there was one young and passable-looking gallant, who occupied his entire dance with me by talking of you, and not content with that,

he resumed the fascinating topic when he claimed
me for a second. I had never met your cousin before, but his remarks convinced me he is a man of
taste."

It was Rose's turn to look out of countenance,
but merriment got the better of her, and she instantly plunged into laughing abuse of Murray,
which would have rejoiced his soul to hear, and
Madam Telfair, for the first time, wondered in her
heart whether it was wise to have that young
gentleman come so frequently and familiarly to
Dumblane.

The pleasant chat flowed on, for although Geraldine was possessed with the uneasy consciousness
that no doubt in a few hours Rose and her mother
would hear of the duel and of Roy's escape, she
could not bring herself to inform them of it;
looking at it in any light it was neither wise nor
prudent for her to do so, and finally bidding Madam
Telfair farewell the two girls walked down the
avenue together, Jumbo following with the horses,
and Rose, longing with all her heart to speak of
Roy, was withheld by fear of incautious meddling
in what she felt was the happiness of her brother's
life. But suddenly Geraldine stopped short in the
path, and laying her hand in Rose's, said softly : —

"I do not know when I may see you again, dear,
or what you may hear said of me and the events
that seem to be crowding each other in my life,
but — Rose, promise me that you will trust me,
and — and — make those you love trust me also if
you can."

" I promise," said Rose, in her low, steadfast voice.

" I am sore bestead; I am pressed on every side. My father is, you know, a stern man and accustomed to be obeyed. He has none but me, and to go against his plans, matured for some years, will vex him sorely. But, Rose, when my own heart speaks — Oh, I am talking in enigmas — you cannot know what I mean, and honor ties my tongue."

" I guess more than you think," whispered Rose, as she saw a brilliant flush dye the fair face.

Geraldine hurried on as the horses came nearer. " Roy thinks he has cause to despise me, alas ! I must leave my vindication to time " — Jumbo stood at her elbow, and in a second Geraldine was in her saddle. But she bent down for a parting kiss, and as she gave it, she breathed softly in Rose's ear, " Tell Roy to trust me still," and was off before Rose could answer.

As Geraldine galloped back down the avenue to the main road she felt a throb of hope. But would Roy understand; could he be so blind as not to know that her apparently cruel speech of the night before was said for Tarleton's ears, because she knew he was close enough to catch her words, and that the knowledge that Roy had been and still was her lover was sufficient to transform him from vague suspicion to unrelenting enmity? Oh, luckless fate, for her coldness had apparently precipitated all she had tried to avoid !

Jumbo and she turned out of the avenue and were proceeding at a moderate pace toward Glenmoira when they caught the sound of horse's feet coming rapidly behind them, and looking back Geraldine saw Tarleton riding after her. Her first feeling was one of thankfulness that he had not chanced to encounter her as she came out from Dumblane, her next was to steady her nerves, and determine that he should be kept at arm's length in his suit by whatever device might come to her.

" A bright morning after our festivities," he said, sweeping her a graceful salute with his plumed hat, for Tarleton always rode faultlessly attired, and his grace and ease were part of his fascinating manner to women ; " you look as fresh as the day itself. I waited, hoping to have the honor of being your escort back to the plantation, as Colonel Moncriffe told me he should be detained, but when I returned from a necessary errand they told me you had taken horse."

" Yes, riding seemed preferable to driving. After dancing it was ever my aunt's custom in London to bid me go for a gallop."

" I have not yet had opportunity to ask how you enjoyed your ball. Indeed I was so annoyed by my enforced absence when in pursuit of that insolent rebel that I scarce had my wits about me for the remainder of the evening."

" You could hardly have been more annoyed than I," said Geraldine coldly.

" Annoyed ! " he began eagerly ; then glancing

at her still, proud face, he changed his tone. " Do you mean that you did me the grace to miss me, or have I had the great misfortune to annoy you ? "

" Surely Colonel Tarleton can hardly consider that he complimented me by making me the object of a broil — a hand-to-hand combat! We are now affording the gossips of Savannah a fruitful topic, no doubt."

" But, madam," cried Tarleton, in absolute dismay, as the red blood rushed into his face, " you are surely aware that I was subjected to the ignominy of a blow, — I, Banastre Tarleton, — and that instant satisfaction was imperative. Permit me to remind you that I came to your rescue as well, from importunities that seemed to offend you."

" I am quite able to defend myself, sir," said his tormentor, " 't is the publicity of the affair that distracts me. How could you bring me into such unenviable notoriety ? " and Geraldine turned her beautiful eyes reproachfully upon him, thereby completing his bewilderment.

" Do you mean that I should again have permitted that insolent rebel to make his escape without endeavor to stay him? He is hardly worth the discussion between you and me, but if he is the cause of your coldness to me this morning, I can find it in my heart to hate him even more than before. Let him look to himself when next he meets Tarleton," and he smothered the oath that came readily to his lips. " Forgive me ; I have startled you, and let me make my peace, or this will be the most wretched day of my existence."

" Then let it pass," said Geraldine gently, and having thus reduced the hitherto invincible Tarleton to abject despair, she allowed him to dismount her as they drew up their horses before the door of Glenmoira.

CHAPTER XIV

UNDER WHICH COLORS

COLONEL MONCRIFFE sat in his library, turning over a pile of papers with hasty hand and frowning brow. His was usually a calm, almost stern demeanor, but it was very evident that something had occurred to ruffle him, for after reading the same letter thrice in succession, he threw it from him, and leaning forward touched the hammer of a gong upon his table sharply. Jupiter, whose duty it was to answer the colonel's summons, came with sufficient speed only to find his master in the act of ringing the second time almost before the first call had died away.

" Tell your mistress I desire her to come to me at once," and Jupiter vanished before what he felt was a coming storm ; or, as he expressed it to Margot, to whom he delivered the message, " Marse been takin' counsel wif de debbil, suah ; bes' not keep him waitin'. " Which translated by Margot reached Geraldine as, " The colonel 's in the library, my leddy, an' somewhat warm ; ye 'll be needin' a' your coolness, so dinna fash yoursel'. "

Geraldine's color mounted, and there was a sparkle in her blue eyes which told of high courage as she went swiftly along the gallery. She was aware that Tarleton and her father had been closeted for more than an hour, and that in all probability she could no longer postpone a decision of some sort as regarded his pretensions.

"You sent for me, father," she said softly, as closing the door she entered his presence. And then she sat down calmly in a high-backed, carved chair, and awaited the storm.

Nothing could have been so disconcerting as this, and Colonel Moncriffe bit his lip, and began the conversation in far more moderate tones than he had intended. This was not the child who had left him three years before, whom he could control by a frown or a sharply spoken word, but a woman with self-possession that equaled if it did not exceed his own. "I have somewhat to say to you, my daughter, in continuation of the subject I broached soon after your return. I then laid before you a plan — the dearest of my life, I think — which involves your future and I may add your happiness. I have made this province my abode; here I met my life's sorrow, the loss of your mother, and three charming boy infants, who might have lived to become the prop of my declining years. Alas! death has left me but you — and on you depends my future to a greater extent than perhaps you can understand." His voice trembled, he was a consummate actor, and he was playing his rôle to win, — the stakes being a child's happiness or misery versus his own comfort and good

name. It must be confessed that Geraldine had
never regarded her father, a man in the very prime
of life, as in immediate need of a prop of any kind,
and she surveyed him with a look of bewilderment
which he interpreted in his own way.

"You doubtless are aware that Colonel Tarleton has fallen monstrously in love with you — a
climax which, though I hoped for, I did not consider necessary, as experience has taught me that
matrimonial connections are happier when formed
with good judgment and regard than those of
highly wrought passion. But this is immaterial;
may I ask your feeling toward your suitor? I
trust you have arrived at a point where the question is not premature."

"Most assuredly not, but it is unfortunate that
Colonel Tarleton has conceived such violent admiration for me, as, save for his handsome looks
and fine manners, he does not appeal to me in the
least."

"Geraldine!" Her father's voice deepened
ominously, and she braced herself again as she
recognized it. "Surely you are not mawkish
enough to desire to fall in love with a husband?"

"I confess to a prejudice in favor of that emotion," she said. "Father, I am by no means ready
to marry any one. Colonel Tarleton, I am aware,
does me much honor. Coming from England,
from scores of titled beauties whom Lady Dolly
assures me have smiled upon him in vain, he seeks
an American with whom he has not one thought

in common. You sent me to England to be
educated, to learn English ways, English ideas,
and (I now understand) to marry an Englishman.
I may have acquired the way, the manner of a
court, but deep down in my heart I am every inch
an American." She paused, her color rose, and
she went on more rapidly. "Dear father, now
that I have come home, I realize what the ever-
recurring want has been during my life in England. In Scotland I had the home-feeling more,
for I love my clan, and the tales of my gallant
ancestors found a responsive throb in my heart each
time I heard them. But here, ah, here, where I
was born, is the sole spot on earth where I can be
happy, and I know now that the ambitions and
glitter of a court can never, never satisfy me.
Thank Colonel Tarleton for the distinguished
honor he has paid me, but let me stay here and live
and die in my own beautiful land of the South."

As Geraldine's voice rang out with its pathetic
pleading her father's face changed from surprise to
fury, and when she ceased he was absolutely livid.

"So, girl," he said under his breath, "you are
an American ; are you likewise a rebel — or a patriot, as their jargon has it? for your high-flown
sentiments need go but one step farther to make
you discard the colors of the king."

"Father ! "

"Ay, and perhaps you are making ready to
take it. That I should live to hear my daughter's
proud name linked with an outlaw-raider! 'T is

common gossip in the city how at the governor's fête a duel was fought for your hand "—

"Stop!" The tone was haughty and inflexible as his own. "I can guard and protect my own dignity even when my father stoops to use such language to his child."

Moncriffe gasped for breath, and for a moment Geraldine thought he would raise his hand and strike her. There was not a sound except his labored breathing, and a sensation of terror crept over the girl, as she watched him until the spasm of fury passed. When he finally spoke he had regained his color, and something of his usual manner.

"In my anger, drawn forth by your contumacious behavior, I have said more than I should," he continued, with cold, but stately courtesy. "I withdraw the epithet I used, but I have now to lay my commands upon you. This match with Colonel Tarleton has the sanction of his father as well as yours; you will accept him, and when the time arrives go with him to the altar."

"Never!" Geraldine sprang from her seat as she spoke, but suddenly, before she could utter another syllable, her father stretched out both hands towards her, tears actually streaming down his face.

"Geraldine, my child," he cried in a voice of agony, "forbear! Take time, put him to the test; ask any terms you please — but do not deprive me of life itself by disobeying my request."

Bewildered, alarmed, with an undefinable sense
of some mystery that she could not penetrate,
Geraldine paused, her eyes filled with terror.
Could she but have read a letter hidden beneath
that pile of papers on the desk before her, she
would have appreciated the cleverness of the act-
ing whose real motive was selfish, calculating con-
cern for his own ends and purposes alone.

"Father, I do not understand your meaning.
How can I promise to do what I never intend to
perform?   Would you counsel me to put such an
insult upon Colonel Tarleton as to pretend that I
will bestow my hand upon him, and then withdraw?"

"No, no," he cried still wildly, as he thought he
perceived that it was possible to carry his point,
"not that, but women have been known to change
their minds, and "—

"What would you have me do?"   Still the
sense of alarm was strong within her; she could
not account for it.

"Only this," he took her hand and pressed it
fondly; "say to him that you will consider the
matter, but there shall be no haste, that you do not
know your own heart "—

"Alas, I read it but too well," murmured Geraldine to herself, but she answered, "If Colonel
Tarleton be willing to take such reply in all
earnestness "—

"He is here to make answer for himself," said
Moncriffe, rising suddenly and throwing open the

door of his private cabinet, where Tarleton had been concealed during the entire interview, although out of hearing. "I will not anticipate him."

"Then, mistress of Tarleton's heart, you will grant my prayer and make me the happiest of men," cried Tarleton, advancing toward her, and at the same moment bestowing a private malediction upon Moncriffe for remaining as witness to the interview, which indeed, for special reasons of his own, that personage did not dare to have transpire except in his presence.

"Nay, you would be of all men most miserable were I to consent at present," said Geraldine, now fully convinced that there was something beneath the surface, and that for the moment she had best appear to yield, "but as I have told you already, I desire time, and, at some later day, perhaps"— And then while Tarleton fell to kissing her hand with rapturous thanks, and her father raised his eyes to Heaven in hypocritical gratitude, Geraldine was saying to herself, "Oh, Roy, Roy, forgive me for the subterfuge," and presently excused herself, and with outward calmness, but inward tumult, went quietly back to her own room, leaving the two men together.

"Faith," said Tarleton, flinging himself on a chair, "you are a man of your word. Leave the rest to me, sir; I can usually bend a woman's will to mine."

"Whether you do or not, my word is pledged,"

returned Moncriffe grimly, thinking how he would destroy that letter the moment he was free to do so.

Margot, going into her young mistress's chamber a little later, found her sobbing bitterly with her face pressed against the pillows of her bed.

"My bairn, my bairn," cried the Scotchwoman, "whatever has befallen ye? Dinna greet; there 'll be happier days to come."

"Not for me, perhaps," said Geraldine despairingly, "but come what may, Margot, one thing is sure. From this day forth I wear the rebel blue, and God save the cause of freedom!"

"I knew it wad come, sooner or later," said Margot; "'t is the bluid — your mither's bluid whilk comes bounding in your veins. Ah, dinna I tell ye that Maister Roy"—

"Hush! do not name him now, for my heart is torn. Listen, Margot," and she related her interview with her father, and its result.

"An' did he greet, an' ca' on Heaven, and fright ye sair? Ah, the villain; forgie me, my leddy, but I hae seen him do the self-same trick wi' your mither, and I ken weel his ways."

"Margot, what do you mean? Tell me, I implore you."

"Not noo; the time 's not ripe, but bide a wee, an' some day I 'll tell ye a'." And with that assurance Geraldine dried her eyes, and rose to dress for supper, for in the days of our grandmothers, as now in ours, they hid their heartaches under laughter and smiles, and quenched their tears with a repartee.

Margot was standing in the servants' quarters some two hours later, giving out supplies from the storeroom, when she heard the trooper, Burt, come whistling softly along the corridor.

" Is that you, Mistress Margot ? " said he, stopping to survey the row of shining black faces, which smiled back at him good-humoredly, for Tarleton's orderly had made himself very popular among the dusky part of the household during his stay on the plantation. " Sugar and coffee, too ; you 'll grow fat on such liberal provision, Aunt Venus."

" 'T ain't likely," retorted the goddess of the kitchen, surveying her portly person with satisfaction ; " reckon dis chile 'bout reached de line fer her time ob life, an' she 's boun' to keep it, ef so be yo' don' hab no mo' battles an' raidin' roun' dis yere plantation to skeer de life outen us. De Lawd knows I ain't lackin' fer hospertalerty, but de sooner we sees de backs ob soldiers, raidcoats or green, it don' matter which, de sweeter will be sleep an' res' fer Venus."

Burt laughed, as the line of blacks trooped away, Aunt Venus leading them, and then he turned toward Margot with a change of face. " I have somewhat to say to you," he said under his breath ; " come outside for a moment ; I distrust brick walls," and Margot, comprehending, motioned him to go before her, and then followed him back of the quarters, where they stopped under a myrtle tree.

"I have something here for your mistress, which came to my hand from a Dutch boy who was riding a horse I happened to know. Use care, Mistress Margot," and he pressed a scrap of paper into her hand, and walked off whistling in the direction of the stables.

Margot looked down dubiously at it, as she proceeded back up the staircase. "Will it hurt or please her?" she thought. "I dinna ken the ways o' these young sweethearts; ane day cruel, ane day kind. But perhaps 't will set her mind at rest ane way or t'ither."

What would sage old Margot have said had she read the few unsigned words on that soiled bit of paper, which her young mistress held in her hand that night as she fell into sweeter sleep than had yet visited her eyes? For the writing, in a hurried, cramped hand, ran: "I have penetrated your ruse; courage, till we meet again."

CHAPTER XV

ON THE TRAIL OF THE SWAMP FOX

It was the close of a hot August day, and the Southern night, which always falls more swiftly than in Northern latitudes, was softly obscuring the landscape not far from where the Santee River wound its way. In the dim light one could still distinguish groups of men, horses, and a train of baggage-wagons with mules tied near them, while here and there was the light of a campfire where the men were cooking fish and making coffee. The command was of goodly size, composed of Georgia loyalists and Tarleton's legion, and for several months they had been engaged in scouring the country in search of Marion, who, having scored a brilliant victory over Frazier at Parker's Ferry, was now engaged in harrying Tarleton, often marching, mounted on the fleet horses which the patriots brought to his aid, sixty miles between sundown and daybreak, striking blows now here, now there, until the British began to regard the Swamp Fox with nameless terror as a mysterious foe, who was always at hand when least expected, with his terrible shout and overwhelming charge. In short, no romance of the Middle Ages excelled this partisan warfare, which, on account of the cruelties employed by the British after the occupation of Charleston and Savannah, was conducted with far more bitterness and revenge than any other part of the war of independence.

In his tent, with Halleck and several other officers, sat Tarleton, resting after many hours spent in the saddle, for having received what appeared to him reliable information, he had made a forced march from the Black River, where he had encamped the day before, to his present position. His camp chest was open, and Burt had just fetched fresh bottles of wine from the sutler's cart, but though jest and mirth filled the tent, Tarleton's brow was moody and his air impatient.

"That innocent, stupid-looking lout whom we found on the river-bank had an eye for a comfortable camping-ground," said Halleck, leaning over as Tarleton refilled his glass in silence.

"Ay, but I am not so sure of its safety," muttered his friend, "therefore I took the precaution to ride fully a mile further than he indicated. These pestilent Whigs have a way of transforming themselves from soldiers into peaceful-looking husbandmen in a fashion that I believe they borrow from the devil himself. Do you recollect the farmer on the Pedee River?"

"Who almost led us into ambush? Ay, but his punishment was swift and sure."

"I made certain of that," replied Tarleton grimly, "for I gave the thrust with my own hand;

he did not need a second. Gascoigne," addressing a young officer of the group, "see that the sentries are placed close along the line of approach from the river; I am somewhat uneasy to-night."

"Yes, colonel," said the man addressed, saluting, as he cast an unconscious glance of regret toward the glass he set down unemptied.

"And return, Gascoigne; we need you to reduce this bottle," said Tarleton, more good-humoredly, with that comradeship which made him a favorite with his friends and those thrown in close companionship with him.

"Tarleton," said Halleck in a low voice, as the others continued the discussion for a moment interrupted, "what news did Burt fetch you? I knew, or rather guessed, what his three days' absence from the command probably meant, but from your careworn brow I fear he brought you somewhat of ill-tidings."

"You are right; affairs at Glenmoira do not appear to progress; in fact I think the lady grows more cold each time I receive a missive — if indeed I be so fortunate as to have reply to mine, which is not always. Halleck, I sometimes think I am indeed bewitched, for the less my passion has to thrive upon, the more mad it grows."

Halleck eyed him for a moment with a half-whimsical smile. "'T is opposition which feeds the flame; your conquests have been all too easy heretofore, man. And then, I grant you, Mistress Moncriffe is wondrous beautiful, and possesses a charm all her own of sweet graciousness."

"And playfulness, and humor, and wit — oh, ay, I can run the gamut of all her witcheries, I promise you. But for me, Halleck, she cares as little as the thistledown that the wind wafts across her path."

"Then why pursue the affair further? There be others " —

"No," cried Tarleton impetuously, "to me there is but the one woman in the universe."

"To-day, — but to-morrow — ?" Halleck hesitated, for he saw the spark of anger light Tarleton's dark eyes.

"I tell you," he said in accents of concentrated passion, "not all the powers of this world or the next can change my purpose. I care not whether she comes to my arms a willing bride or no — possess her I will, or " —

Out on the still night air there rang a sudden shot, followed by a distant shout, which was repeated from sentry to sentry. Tarleton sprang to his feet and snatched his sword from the spot where he had flung it down, and in a second the party were outside the tent, where they were met by Gascoigne.

"The shot came from the sentry furthest west," said he. "Hark! the picket-guard are advancing this way," and through the bushes came a line of soldiers with some one in their midst.

"A prisoner," cried Tarleton eagerly, his eyes beginning to sparkle with the excitement of coming strife. The group of officers peered intently into the gloom, as the guard filed in sight, and the corporal, saluting, pressed forward.

"I have to report a prisoner, sir, who endeavored to land and cross our lines from a canoe which she had evidently paddled down the river" —

"She!" echoed Tarleton, as the slim, straight figure of an Indian girl stepped forward with a trooper on either side. "Whom have we here? Bring her inside my tent," and he walked leisurely back, signing Halleck to accompany him. Entering, he took a pine torch, and cast its light full upon the girl, who stood unmoved beneath his scrutiny.

"My princess of the woods!" cried Tarleton, suddenly recognizing Laceola. "By gad, Halleck, she has wandered far to find me this time. Search her," to the guard, "and be sure she has no weapons."

"Apparently none, sir," said the soldier, while Burt came forward and stood behind her, obedient to a sign from Tarleton; "there was a pistol in her belt which the sentry secured. That was the shot you heard; she was trying to escape."

"You may go," said Tarleton after a pause, during which he eyed Laceola intently, and the guard left the tent. The flickering light of the pine torch fell aslant the girl's face, but she might have been a statue save for her breathing, so motionless was she, as she stood, her haughty eyes looking beyond the inmates of the tent, in silence.

"What brings you here?" asked Tarleton, breaking the stillness sharply.

" The redcoat soldiers dragged Laceola; she had no wish to come."

" Answer my question; what brought you on the river? "

" Laceola goes on her way toward the setting sun. Her home is beyond the Great River; let her return undisturbed to her people."

" Not until I am satisfied that you are not a spy; have you not been with Marion's forces? "

" The lair of the Swamp Fox is many miles away on an island where there are no bridges for the redcoats to cross," said Laceola contemptuously.

" Can you direct us on the trail? If we can but locate the spot, girl, I will reward you well."

" Laceola's eyes are keen, but she cannot see far enough to show the road to the soldiers of the king."

" In other words, you will not. Beware, I am not to be trifled with, and I do not choose to *hold* prisoners." It did not need the deadly menace of his tone to convey his meaning, for his sinister glance was interpreted both by the Indian girl and Halleck, and the latter said hastily under his breath: " Better powwow, Tarleton; you may persuade, but I fear you cannot drive this piece of femininity. Let me try."

Something in the girl's fearless eye made Tarleton pause, and Halleck addressed her in softer voice. " Has Laceola seen the Swamp Fox this moon? Does he ride with many men? "

" Some days many, some days few. Did not

the redcoats find him on the banks of the Pedee ? "

" Ay, curse you ! " cried Tarleton, stung by the
reference, " 't is useless parleying with the jade
longer. We could not trust her even as guide,
and she might lead us into ambush. Oh, could I
but capture this wily Marion — hark ! more trouble
along the line," for a rushing, murmuring sound
came on the wind. " See to it that the girl does
not elude you this time, Burt. What 's that ?
Good God ! the enemy ! "

Well might Tarleton shout " To horse ! " as he
tore out of the tent, followed by Halleck, for on
his left and in his rear were dashing lines of riders
led by the invincible Marion himself, and out
above the clash and din, as the surprised British
endeavored to rally and charge, came the hoarse
battle-cry of the patriots, —

" No quarter for Tories ! Remember Waxhaw
Creek ! "

Laceola laid her hand on Burt's arm, as he
sprang to follow Tarleton. " Laceola's shot was
the signal to the Swamp Fox," she whispered
breathlessly. " He had been watching for the
British from yonder morass since morning, and
Laceola paddled her canoe softly down the river
till she came where the sentry stood. Bounding
Elk said Laceola must speak soft words until she
heard the horses' hoofs rush from behind."

" By heavens, girl, you did your trick well !
I 'll not detain you," and extinguishing the pine

torch he rushed out into the fight followed by the
Indian girl.

Outside was wild tumult and confusion; the
deadly ring of the sharpshooters' bullets, the rifle
volleys, shouts, shrieks, and groans, as horses and
men went down before that wild charge of Marion's
men. Frequently had that redoubtable leader attacked the enemy at night, and it was said that the
patriots as well as their trusty beasts could see as
clearly by night as by day, and this added to the
terror which they inspired. In vain did Tarleton
and Halleck, with scores of other officers, try to
rally their command; the rout went on, and sore-
pressed, fighting bravely in his rage and mortification, Tarleton finally made good his escape with
a handful of his legion, and reached the banks of
the Edisto River as dawn broke over the forests.[1]

To Marion and his gallant band the sun rose
joyously, for beside as many prisoners as they could
safely manage to carry with them, they had captured Tarleton's baggage train, and it may be
readily imagined with what delight those men who
had for months subsisted on the most meagre diet
welcomed a return to food in plenty. And safely
ensconced in a friendly swamp, which afforded
them ample concealment and means of escape in
case of attack, they indulged in the almost forgotten luxuries of sugar, tea, coffee, and even pep-

---

[1] In this engagement at midnight, Marion lost one man killed;
the Tories were almost annihilated. (Lossing's *Field Book of the
Revolution.*)

per, with an appetite which threatened to make large inroads into their newly acquired stores.

On the log of a fallen live oak sat Roy Telfair, talking busily with McKay, as they ate their breakfast, with an air of elation which they had fairly earned the right to enjoy.

"Faith, Telfair, those British know how to provide for their comfort," said McKay, stirring the unwonted sugar in his pewter pannikin of coffee. "This is an improvement on our herb tea, which, even with a dash of cognac in it, was hardly palatable."

"Ay, and the river fish never tasted as good as with this sprinkle of pepper," taking a liberal pinch of that condiment from an oak leaf where he had bestowed it. "It gives one rather a homesick feeling for the nonce, McKay; perhaps 't is as well for us that we have a few hardships in the way of subsisting on what we forage for ourselves in the forest. 'T is a strong, hardy life, and for one, I 've grown to love it well."

"And so have I," returned McKay heartily, "but I hear rumor has it that we are ordered to join the new general, Gates, whom the commander in chief has sent to superintend the campaign in the South."

"Pray Heaven he may be a better one than our last. Who 's this coming over the grass in our direction?" Both officers looked up to see Ossaba, followed by Laceola, approaching them, while from the other side came an orderly who addressed Telfair.

" Colonel Marion desires that Captain Telfair and Captain McKay come to him for conference at once. He is a few yards to the right, beyond the wagons."

" Laceola will wait," said the Indian girl, as Roy turned courteously towards her before departing on the errand. "Ossaba and Laceola are to scout; the Bounding Elk will hear the Swamp Fox's words and return," and folding her blanket across her breast Laceola seated herself calmly on the ground as Telfair and McKay went hastily in response to Marion's summons.

They found their leader in full conclave with his officers, and as they approached he beckoned the young men to his side.

" I sent for you, gentlemen, to thank you for your personal prowess of last night, and to inform you that I am ordered to report, with such of my command as I can gather, to General Gates, just appointed to take the field in the Carolinas. I shall therefore push on to join him near Camden with all possible dispatch, but I deem it necessary that a small force be left to hang upon the British flanks between this and the Savannah River. Therefore I shall detach some two hundred men, leaving you, Captain McKay, in command, with Telfair as your second, and detach two of the Indian scouts to accompany you, as they are of great service in such duty. Take care of your men, gentlemen; beware of surprises (except they be of your own making), and remain upon this duty until further orders. The force will be ready to march by sunset. Farewell, and good fortune attend you till we meet again," and with a warm pressure of the hand and his kindly, almost affectionate smile, Marion dismissed them, and resumed his conversation with his other officers.

McKay and Telfair had a busy day before them, and it was not until it was almost time to start that the latter found time to speak to Laceola, who wandered to and fro, helping the men, who welcomed her warmly, for her good service of the night before had been made rumor in the camp, and Marion himself had commended her.

" We move toward the southwest," said Roy, " and can easily reach the Edisto by the morning. There is a pony for you, Laceola ; Ossaba can take the trail to-night."

" It must be as the Bounding Elk pleases." A swift flush mounted to the girl's face. " Laceola can scout by night or day. Is her place in the front or the rear?"

" In the rear when we start. Are you not tired? Last night's skirmish and march were heavy work."

" Not when the redcoats fall and flee," said the girl proudly, " but the chief-who-loves-blood escaped. Laceola's knife was ready and its blade is keen ; he spoke bad words to Laceola, and she does not forget."

" Tarleton?" cried Telfair amazed. He knew nothing of Laceola's encounter with the British officer, and could imagine no cause for her apparent hatred.

" Laceola was his prisoner as he rode to see the palefaced maiden, — the White Fawn's friend, — but she escaped. The chief-who-loves-blood kissed Laceola on the lips — pah!" and her eyes blazed at recollection of the insult.

" He did!" The swift blood flew to Roy's face. " The base villain, to take advantage of your help- lessness! Would I had been there!"

A soft moisture wet Laceola's eyes as she turned them upon him. " The Bounding Elk's words are good, they fall kindly upon Laceola's ears. Do not fear; Laceola can both shoot and strike," and she laid her hand on her belt as she bent her head and glided swiftly away, for the men were mount- ing, and Roy turned his horse's head toward the column, fuming inwardly at this fresh evidence of Tarleton's profligate ways.

The sun was setting in a golden bank of clouds as the forces separated, Roy and McKay with their little band, and Marion to ride and join Gates, where his ragged and ill-clad soldiers excited de- rision (to his shame be it said) in the new com- mander, and caused him to mistakenly imagine that Marion's men were of small consequence as a fighting factor, and for this reason, on the eve of the battle of Camden, Marion and Horry were sent back on the useless errand of destroying bridges behind the British to prevent their escape. Thus Marion's men were saved to the partisan warfare; a most providential happening for the provinces of South Carolina and Georgia.[1]

It was almost the close of the second day, when McKay and Telfair drew rein, and advised the men to dismount in a glade which appeared as a welcome relief to the forest and undergrowth through which they had been struggling for some miles. But tempting though it looked to the weary riders, Telfair's mind misgave him, and he suggested to McKay that a certain piece of swamp land some five miles further, of which Ossaba informed him, was perhaps a safer, though not so attractive a camping-ground for the night. McKay, usually kindly, was chiefly irascible when in command, and considering this somewhat of a reflection upon his judgment, sharply replied that five miles further would tire both horses and men to no purpose, so Roy wisely kept his temper and said no more. But he was not rendered less uneasy by seeing that Laceola slipped from her pony, and instead of resting or coming to partake of supper, disappeared silently among the trees.

An hour later, nothing seeming to disturb the quiet of the improvised camp, Telfair began to dismiss his distrust of the position, and having eaten his supper, and seeing that the men and horses were equally well supplied, he threw himself on the ground by McKay and resolved to keep awake in the twilight if possible, and await the return of Laceola. But to resolve was one thing;

[1] See contemporaneous histories.

tired nature, which rebelled against three consecu-
tive days in the saddle, another, as Roy found; for
presently, to McKay's secret enjoyment, Telfair
made no answer to a question put to him, and looking around he saw that his friend had fallen fast
asleep, with his head resting against the trunk of
a tree under which they sat. Another hour, and
McKay was meditating upon following Roy's example, when suddenly Laceola came flying at full
speed across the open glade, and between the trees,
dimly seen, were troopers in pursuit.

"Mount! mount!" cried the girl as she rushed
past the men, who, springing up, ran for their horses,
and with incredible swiftness she reached the spot
where Roy's horse was tied. With shouts and
shots the British were upon them, and as Roy
sprang to his feet Laceola thrust the reins in his
hand and darted behind a tree. Volley upon
volley from the British followed, and the Americans, rallying almost instantly from their surprise,
stood bravely to their rifles and returned the fire,
but slowly and sullenly they were forced to retreat
into the brush and down the trail toward the river.
Roy, fighting gallantly, at last was compelled to
follow his men, but as he backed his horse, in the
act of firing, a shot struck him in the side, and he
fell headlong from the saddle, rolling under the
horse. That animal (a finely bred hunter, in the
days before Roy joined Marion) stood still, and
Roy looked about him for a chance of escape.
Alas, it seemed but small, for the British (a com-

mand, as he afterwards found, who were marching
from Charleston to join Tarleton) far outnumbered
the Americans, and should he give sign of life he
had little doubt he would be put to the sword, as
many of the troopers had dismounted, and were
apparently engaged in slaughter.   Suddenly his
horse, already roused by the gleam of steel, and
the whistle of bullets which still continued, began
to prick its ears and show every sign of excitement ;
what if he could cling to its neck and so be borne
from the fray ?   The thought had hardly passed
through Roy's brain, when floating on the breeze
came the faint notes of the American bugler sounding " retreat."   With a supreme effort (for he was
beginning to feel the loss of blood attendant upon
his wound) Roy raised himself and flung both arms
around the good beast's neck as the horse, with
ears erect and nostrils distended, started to gallop
in the direction of the call.   A leap, a bound, —
they were halfway across the glade, the horse
dashing with greater speed as he passed over the
wounded who lay on the ground ; another effort,
heightened in its swiftness by shots from a trooper
who stood in the path of the now thoroughly terrified animal, and with a loud neigh, as if to answer
the call he knew so well, the horse and his master
dashed on through the British ranks, and in a few
seconds more were far beyond pursuit, heading gallantly for their comrades.

Roy closed his eyes ; the excitement of his
strange rescue over, he began to wonder if his

strength would hold out until they could reach his retreating command. Fainter and fainter he grew; he tried to speak to the horse, but words seemed denied him, and only gasps came from his lips. Finally, he felt his arms relax, and a thrill of horror passed over him as he realized that he might be trampled upon by those flying hoofs; then he heard as in a dream a faint cry, the horse stopped as a hand grasped the bridle, and Roy fell senseless upon the grass beneath him.

CHAPTER XVI

LACEOLA'S first effort after backing the horse from Roy's prostrate body was to secure that animal to the nearest tree, then she knelt down beside Roy and succeeded in stanching the blood which flowed from his wound, by tearing a strip from her blanket and binding it snugly around his arm and shoulder, and after a few minutes of terror and anxiety she had the satisfaction of seeing him open his eyes.

" It is you, Laceola," he said faintly ; " where are the others ? "

" Far away on the southern trail ; is the Bounding Elk able to raise himself ? If so, Laceola will mount him on the saddle and ride behind him to a place of safety."

" How did you come here, and where are we ? "

" Laceola had crept, Indian fashion, to cover, and when she saw the Bounding Elk pass her hanging to the horse's neck she ran swiftly in the same direction ; Laceola is fleet, and no one saw her. The British were too busy with the wounded to follow, and the horse knew Laceola's voice and stopped when she caught the bridle."

"I owe you my life, Laceola, for I recollect thinking I could not hold on an instant longer."

"But the Bounding Elk must not tarry here; we are too near, and a scout may find us."

"Ay," said Roy, making an effort to rise and sinking instantly back. "I fear you will be obliged to leave me here, for I seem utterly spent. Drag me into the bushes there, and go in search of some of the men. I can manage by myself, no doubt, until it be safe for you to bring me aid." But even as he uttered the brave words, Roy knew that the chances were about even that he would perish by loss of blood, or at the hand of some merciless camp-follower, who might give him a finishing stroke, if only to plunder the sword he wore.

Laceola looked at him for a moment in silence; then she went swiftly to the horse and untied him, and bringing him to the decayed stump of a tree not many feet from the spot where Roy had fallen, she threw the reins on his neck, as he had been trained to stand, and went back to Roy.

"Let the Bounding Elk put his hand on Laceola's shoulder as she creeps by his side, and she will guide him to the stump, yonder: from the stump, she can lift him to the saddle. Laceola is young and strong."

But she spoke to almost deaf ears, and realizing how precious time was, the Indian girl stooped, and clasping the almost senseless man in her arms, half carried, half dragged him the few feet she knew

were necessary for his safety.   As she did so she
felt something hard press against her arm, and
putting her hand inside his coat pulled forth a
pocket flask of leather, and, to her great relief, she
found that it contained a small amount of liqueur.
Panting and almost breathless from her exertion,
she propped Roy's head against the friendly stump,
and held the flask to his lips.   To her dismay, at
first the cognac seemed to trickle down outside his
mouth, but by holding his head farther back, she
succeeded in getting a few drops between his teeth,
and finally after swallowing a mouthful, he opened
his eyes and revived.

"I thank you," smiling bravely up into the anxious face bending over him; "that puts some life
into me.   Perhaps — I may — try to mount" —

"Bounding Elk must not talk — some one may
hear, — hush!" panted the girl, as she heard a
rustle in the bushes, but it was only a jack-rabbit,
which gazed at the pair with its bright, surprised
eyes as it sped hurriedly away, and recovering herself Laceola brought the horse close to Roy's side.
After giving him a little more cognac he was able
to raise himself; at last with one brave effort he
struggled once more into the saddle, and with a
bound Laceola mounted behind him.   Throwing
her arms around him as she caught the reins, they
were away, but walking the good horse slowly, both
for fear of noise attracting attention from out-
lying scouts, and because a more rapid motion
might start the bleeding again.

They traveled thus for more than a half hour, Laceola guiding the horse with unerring skill, but at last Roy began to lean more and more heavily upon her, and she realized that he must be speedily laid down and his wound dressed, or worse might ensue. Like every Indian, Laceola knew a few simple and effective means of relieving him, and after peering anxiously along, as the late moon came up in the sky and gave her more light as guide, she apparently discovered what she was seeking, for with a relieved sigh and a few muttered words in her own tongue, she plunged out of the main trail which they were following, and struck off toward the northwest. Still on, and the path grew more rocky; they seemed to be making an ascent as of a hill, and at last, when about halfway to its summit, Laceola checked the horse and threw herself off its back just in time to receive Roy's fainting form as it slipped from the saddle into her outstretched arms.

Then followed a long, long night to Roy Telfair. In it he seemed to see strange forms and places; now he was wandering through a forest with Laceola in search of game, then he seemed to be in a high, vaulted room with white marble pillars, which closed above his head like the arches of some grand cathedral. The light seemed dim, and was that Geraldine, that graceful form which seemed to flit in and out of this dome-like place? Was this the choir of an English church, or a palace where he was imprisoned? And then off again

into wild fever and delirium, when all he was con-
scious of was a cool hand laid on his brow, or a
drop of water that moistened his parched mouth.
But there came a day when he opened his brave,
sunny eyes and saw and knew the world again.

When he came to himself he was lying on a
heap of dried moss and leaves, and, as he felt these
with trembling fingers, his hand came in contact
with something like a blanket.   His eyes, growing
accustomed to the light (and even that was somewhat dim, as it came from a distant torch out of
the range of his vision), saw above him the high
vault of a cavern, — but what a cavern, — for the
air seemed sufficiently clear and pure, — and there
were the strange pillars which had haunted his
dreams, of pure white, and, where the light struck
them, glittering like snow in the sunlight.   As
Roy's mind slowly and gropingly took in these singular details, with the sudden flash that sometimes illuminates the brain after long torpor, he
realized his surroundings, and knew that he must
be lying within one of the curious and beautiful
saltpetre caves of which he had often heard, but
which he had never seen.[1]

As he turned his head he uttered a faint sound,
and from the foot of one of the stalactite pillars
he saw Laceola rise and come swiftly toward him.
Joy beamed in her dark eyes as she said in a voice
that trembled with feeling, —

[1] For description of saltpetre caves, see *Historical Collections
of Georgia.*

" The Bounding Elk has come back to life once more; does he know Laceola?" and with an indescribably graceful yet pathetic gesture she took his hand and carried it to her lips.

" Laceola, what have you done for me, and why am I here?"

" Does the Bounding Elk remember how he was shot, and then the horse brought him away? He has been ill with fever."

" How long? and did you take care of me, Laceola? I recollect that ride, but I do not remember coming to this place. How did you find it?"

" Laceola's tribe know many of these caves. Some of them, far away toward the north, are places where her people meet for dances or councils. This is smaller than most; it has but two rooms; see, there is where we came in," and she pointed to a low passage-way; " the horse is there beyond; he was too tall to crawl through the narrow way where Laceola brought the Bounding Elk inside the cave."

" But tell me, quickly, what ails me? where is the bullet, which I remember struck my shoulder?"

" There was no bullet left in the Bounding Elk; it tore his shoulder, but it did not lodge there. Laceola knew how to treat the wound; there are leaves growing on the hillside which she laid on it, and it is healed. And she gave him herbs to drink, and they cooled the fever. He has been here for two moons and a day."

"Almost two months!" cried Roy in dismay. "How did you live — are you not starving?"

Laceola shook her head, and her smile deepened. "The Bounding Elk forgets that Laceola can shoot and fish. The river is not far away and there is a spring on the hillside."

"And my horse — did you not say he was here also? How did you continue to feed him?"

"That was easy; there is always grass, and Laceola feared to let him graze outside lest the cave be discovered by those who might harm the Bounding Elk, so she gathered the grass and fed the horse with it."

"How can I ever repay you?" cried Roy, his eyes filling as he heard this simple story of the Indian girl's devotion. "But for you I should be lying dead under the gray moss — food for the buzzards, with none to tell the story of how I died."

Laceola laid her hand on his arm. "Too much talk will make fever; here is food; then Bounding Elk must sleep." Roy watched her curiously as she went through the narrow opening which evidently connected the two compartments of the cave. Presently she returned, bringing, in the leather flask which he recognized as his own, some warm liquid which she put to his lips.

"Do not fear; it is made of the flesh of a rabbit which Laceola trapped. This cave has been once inhabited by my people, long, long ago, for Laceola found a rude earthen pot one day over there by the big white stone, and she was glad, for in it she fetched water from the spring, and warmed it to slake the Bounding Elk's fever. Sleep now," as Roy sank back among the leaves, " Laceola will watch."

That sleep proved the turning-point in Roy's recovery, for when he woke again, which was not for some eight hours, he had improved sufficiently to sit upright, and so Laceola found him when she came in from the other side, hearing him move, and her clear pretty laugh provoked an echo in the cave, and pleased Roy because it was so seldom heard.

After that day Roy improved rapidly, and at last was able to walk slowly about the cave, whose singular beauty had a great attraction for him. The continual drippings of lime and saltpetre had formed by concretion these strangely shaped mounds and columns, and Laceola, returning one day after a brief absence, found him seated and examining them closely.

" I am almost myself again," he said as she entered, stretching out his hands, though a warning twinge in his left shoulder made him regard it somewhat ruefully. " Faith, 't is fortunate I have my sword arm unhurt, and this improves daily ; I believe it only needs exercise. I must not tarry here, Laceola, but get back to my command, though Heaven knows where that may be ; if, as you say, we have been almost two months imprisoned here."

"The Bounding Elk is not yet able to sit his horse; perhaps if Laceola could hold him " —

" No, no," cried Roy, " that I absolutely forbid. When we go forth from this cave I will ride as a man should, and I am able to do it now. I owe more to you than I can ever pay, and I must be off."

" The Bounding Elk owes Laceola nothing," said the girl, in a proud, hurt tone ; " he has more than paid her by his grateful words."

" Nay, I did not mean to wound you ; forgive me."

Laceola looked at him for a moment in silence ; then she seated herself beside him, and with bowed head and clasped hands, began to speak, at first low and faltering, but then in bolder fashion.

" The Bounding Elk knows not all ; he is able now to listen ; let him hear the words of Laceola. When he lay day by day tossing with fever in this cave, some days silent, some days talking, Laceola learned many things. He thought he was roaming with her in the forest, where he shot the game, and Laceola carried it, and was happy. Then for days he walked with the palefaced maiden — she with the hair like sunset, and eyes like the blue waters ; and he prayed and pleaded with her, for love was on his lips and in his heart. And then the heart of Laceola grew hot within her breast, for when she held his hand and bathed his forehead he thought it was that other, and he kissed her hands and said words that pierced the soul of

Laceola." She paused for a moment, and Roy regarded her with absolute consternation, as a conviction of what he must have revealed burst upon him. He was about to speak, but the Indian girl raised her slender hand. "Wait; let the Bounding Elk hear all." Her great soft eyes glowed with sombre fire; never had she been so beautiful or so sad.

"Then as Laceola looked upon him and felt the power of his words, she said within herself, 'Why should the Indian girl save the life which is not for her?'— for, to her shame, Laceola knew that she loved the Bounding Elk and longed for his love in return. And thinking thus she laid him back upon his bed and crept away, leaving him to die. Over there, by the white mound she sat, till the sound of his voice grew faint and weak — then it stopped altogether. Still she sat motionless, until the stillness became too great to bear, and then she crept softly back to his side. One look at his face told her that he was almost in the land of spirits. She cried out in her despair, because Laceola knew at last that for her it was greater pain to lose him than to see him live and know that he loved the beautiful maiden of the palefaces."

Again Roy tried to speak, but she forbade him. "She tore open his coat and felt that his heart still beat, though feebly, and she once again forced the fire-water through his lips, and after a long, long time she brought the almost escaped spirit back to

his body, and the Great Spirit, who had hid his
face from Laceola while evil thoughts had possession of her, smiled upon her effort, and slowly, slowly
life and strength came back to the Bounding Elk.
He will soon be able to tread the forest as of old,
but before he goes will he say 'forgive' to Laceola ? "

She raised her head, her great eyes swimming
in tears, and stretched out her slender hands
toward him ; the passionate, faithful love she bore
him shone in every feature of her speaking face.

" Laceola ! "   Roy's voice trembled, and his love
for Geraldine did not prevent a bitter pang of
regret that all unconsciously he had won a devotion so pure, a love so humble, that it had forced
a confession where none was needed, as her nobility
of soul forbade her to be silent because of her
involuntary treachery, so deeply repented.   " How
can I express my grief that I should have caused
you such pain, how tell you that I "—

" Hush ! "   Laceola sprang forward as the warning left her lips.   Her quick ears had caught a faint
sound in the cave beyond.   She drew Roy's pistol
from her belt, where she had worn it since the
night of the skirmish, and with steady aim she
covered the narrow entrance of the cave.   Another
rustling sound ; the horse whinnied gently ; then
Roy heard the unmistakable tramp of mounted
men, and a dark form came cautiously into view.

" Ossaba ! "   Laceola thrust the pistol aside and
darted forward, and in another second McKay had

made his way through the passage, and was wringing
Roy's hand, talking so rapidly and joyously that
it was at first difficult to understand how or whence
he came.

"We gave you up for lost weeks ago ; indeed, two
of the men declared that they passed you lying
wounded beneath your horse "—

"Ay, so they may have, but Laccola aided my
escape and with wonderful heroism brought me
here."

"Brave girl," cried McKay. "Marion himself
shall thank you."

"But how did you find me, McKay? Did Ossaba bethink himself of this cave?"

"No, we are on a scout ; for since the dire confusion after the battle of Camden (we lost fear-
fully there, Telfair ; but by great good luck Gates
had dispatched the Rangers southward before the
conflict) we have been doing yeoman service at our
old trade of harrying the British all over the province. But as we were passing the foot of this hill
Ossaba declared that he saw Laccola's trail (these
Indians appear to have the instinct of a hound for
friend or foe), and that roused me, for we thought
the girl dead also ; so we came cautiously up, and
at last Ossaba told me he believed there was a
cave midway of the ascent ; we continued to follow him, heard your horse call its fellows, and,
thank God, found both that brave girl and you."

"And what of the cause?" asked Roy, as, some
hours after, the troopers helped him outside, and

he sat down to eat a meal with his comrade, who determined not to push on until he could take Telfair with him. "Fancy my thirst for news, and relieve my suspense."

"Oh, aye; we have changed generals again, and Gates is to be superseded by Greene, a man whom Marion likes and respects for his military ability And by word which reached me last night, who do you think comes to join us of the South? Morgan, the 'Border Eagle' as the Indians call him, — Morgan, who, though invalided and sent home, can no longer hold back, and notwithstanding his notorious ill treatment by the Continental Congress, to his eternal honor, be it told, comes back to the army as colonel, where his services merit that he should be general. You must hasten to make your recovery, man; we have made history these two months past, and we need all good patriots such as you to help us on to victory."

"And my people," questioned Telfair; "can you give me news of them? Do they also believe me dead?"

"They know that you are missing, for Ossaba has lately visited Savannah, and while there he saw your sister. But you can easily relieve their apprehensions now. Faith, I can scarcely yet believe in your good luck in escaping, and my conscience has nearly weighed me down with the burden of thinking that I should have taken your suggestion and gone on to the swamp that night we were surprised. I made a clean breast of it to Colonel Marion, and gave you due credit for advice I was fool enough to reject," and the gallant fellow's voice broke, as he wrung Roy's hand again for the twentieth time.

But next day when McKay realized how serious had been Roy's long suffering, he decided that he could not take him with his command, so he detached four troopers as escort, and dispatched his friend to Snow Island, where in Marion's camp he felt sure he would be far safer than to return to Savannah, as at Dumblane he would be in a position to be captured at any moment by the British. Roy reluctantly agreed to this decision, but before he started he called Laceola to his side.

" Farewell," he said; " remember that I am now and always your debtor for nobility and devotion that I have never known surpassed."

" Then the Bounding Elk forgives ?

The hot color rushed into Roy's pale face; he took the girl's hand and raised it to his lips as reverently as if she had been a princess. " Never name such a thing between you and me. I were less than man did I not feel that you have given me life."

" Farewell," she said gently; " the Wild Pigeon flies southward, and she will bear tidings to those the Bounding Elk loves which will bring light to their eyes and gladness to their hearts. Farewell!" and as Roy rode carefully down the hillside he paused at its foot to look back and wave his hand to the graceful, watching figure standing with her face turned toward the rising sun.

CHAPTER XVII

MARGOT DOES HER DUTY

LADY DOLLY was having her matinée, and what
with her personal charm and popularity, and the
novelty of holding an informal reception at eleven
o'clock in the morning, the drawing-room was
fairly crowded with all the social world of Savannah. True, some carping critics had sneered in a
superior manner when the idea was broached as
being quite the latest mode in London and Paris,
but after the first two of these delightfully informal affairs had passed off successfully, the third
bade fair to include every one who had any pre-
tension to being fashionable, even the critics aforesaid.

Lady Dolly, dressed in the last new negligée
costume, which happened to be a Watteau-shaped
garment of rose-colored satin, with the daintiest of
lace mobcaps crowning her yellow curls, sat at a
three-legged Chippendale table, dispensing chocolate in tiny, priceless cups of Sèvres china, looking very much like a Dresden figure herself.
Allastar Murray stood at her elbow, and Molly
Durbeville occupied a chair at her left, where Ensign Selwyn was whispering in her ear and en-

deavoring to retain the attention of that lively and capricious lady.

"I have not seen you for an age," said Lady Dolly, as Murray ventured to beg for another cup of chocolate; "between my trip to Charleston and various engagements since my return I seem to have lost count of my friends in Savannah. Give me a vivid and particular history of all that has transpired since we met."

"That is hardly possible, for we are too tranquil just now to be interesting; we have actually been some weeks without any warlike episodes near us; surely you had plenty of such in South Carolina?"

"Oh, aye, and that reminds me, I saw Colonel Tarleton one night at a supper monstrous pleased because he had had a skirmish with Sumter and forced him to retire."

"But the Tories have had much the best of it in South Carolina of late, save for your old acquaintances, the followers of the Swamp Fox, who are giving them perpetual trouble."

"That gentleman is well named," said Lady Dolly, laughing; "and that reminds me, has that disappearing rebel, young Telfair, been heard of lately?"

"No, not since the duel in the governor's garden; indeed there is great distress at Dumblane, for Madam Telfair believes him dead."

"Dead!" cried Lady Dolly, shocked into sudden gravity. "Oh, I hope not. So gallant a foe commands my sympathy, and to be frank, Murray,

his escapades savored so much of the romantic that
(shall I own it?) I was naughty enough to rejoice
in his success."

"Oh, fie, Lady Dolly; 'tis well you are whispering to one who knows you so well. What
would all this assembly say to such treasonable
utterances?"

Lady Dolly eyed him with a mischievous smile.
"Rumor has it that you are somewhat bitten with
the same; indeed, I heard a whisper that a fair
lady at Dumblane was answerable for your luke-
warm sentiments in favor of the crown."

Murray flushed scarlet. "Who dares" — he
began hotly. But Lady Dolly laid a pretty hand
on his arm.

"And why not? Love laughs at locksmiths, —
why not at Whigs and Tories? I am, myself,
half touched, half fired by these dashing, brave un-
complaining patriots. Your forbears and mine
were out in the 'Forty-Five;' it occurs to me
that perchance I have a few ounces of rebel blood
somewhere in these blue veins of mine, which
makes them throb in sympathy."

There was a little stir near the door, and as it
swung open Geraldine Moncriffe crossed the threshold. Murray started forward to meet her, and
Lady Dolly motioned her to sit at her side.

"A good day to you," she said warmly, as she
pressed Geraldine's extended hand. "'Tis early
for a trip from Glenmoira, and I am much honored
by your presence at my matinée."

Geraldine murmured her thanks as she accepted a cup of chocolate, and Lady Dolly's keen, bright eyes searched her face with a single rapid glance. What had changed her thus? The lovely rose-tinted skin was beautiful as ever, but in those deep blue eyes there lay a shadow of anguish, and the dark lines beneath told of tears and sorrow. What could have befallen her?

"There is some mystery here," thought Lady Dolly, more grieved than she could have believed herself capable of being, although she called herself a woman of sentiment. "Can Tarleton be responsible for this? He is cruel as the grave, and if jealousy prompts him, a fiend. No, she has too much pride and spirit to submit to that. Oh! I must find out what grieves her, or die of sympathy." The last was Lady Dolly's picturesque method of disguising her insatiate curiosity. Forgive her; we are all prone to seek pretty names for our pet foibles.

In a few seconds there was a little circle surrounding Geraldine, for her popularity had grown since the governor's fête, and beside, the unceasing round of entertaining at Glenmoira was fully appreciated by the Tory element of society. Molly Durbeville and Selwyn joined the circle, and laughter and pretty speeches prevailed until one unlucky woman chanced to remember a tale told last evening by her maid.

"Have you heard the news?" she asked, addressing no one in particular, and yet the conversa-

tion paused at her question. " 'T is quite thrilling
in its details.   There has been a whisper brought
to town (no one knows how, probably by the
blacks) that ever since the battle of Camden,
Captain Roy Telfair has been among the missing.
They say his father caused inquiry to be closely
made, and that it was learned he made his escape
from the battlefield, but being closely set upon by
the British forces, he was recaptured, and so worked
upon by the officer in command that at last he con-
sented to conduct a small party to the secret camp
of Marion, provided his freedom be given him."

" I do not credit it for one instant," cried the
indignant voice of Molly Durbeville.

" But wait until you hear the sequel.   Captain
Telfair, sharing apparently the foxlike attributes
of his commanding officer, carefully led the party
into an ambush, but alack! he did not provide for
his own neck, for he fell pierced by a dozen shots
from the British, and was instantly killed.   They
say the body has not yet been recovered, although
Marion's scouts are searching for it."

" Where did you hear that veracious tale?"
asked Murray, seizing the chocolate cup which almost slipped from Geraldine's trembling fingers,
and thereby screening her emotion from observation.   " I am aware that Telfair has been missing
for some two months (I have it from the family
at Dumblane), but I am sure that gruesome tale
lacks confirmation."

" Trust that elusive young gentleman to make

good an escape," interposed Lady Dolly; she was
positive now from Geraldine's agitation that this
was an affair that appealed to her most romantic
side, and in her heart of hearts, as usual, espoused
the cause of true love and its troubled waters.
" From my own knowledge of him (which, Heaven
save the mark, is but small) I can testify that he
crawls through keyholes and out of barred windows — at least that is what we are all forced to
believe at Glenmoira. Nay, must you go?" as
Geraldine, with an eloquent glance of her expressive eyes, rose to leave. " I shall not fail to come
as I promised to-morrow."

" Let me see you to your chariot," said Murray,
and he followed Geraldine down the staircase to
the door.

" What did Rose say?" she asked, and her
voice was now under sufficient control to be steady;
" had they any further tidings of Captain Telfair ? "

" Only what you have heard, but truly we must
make large allowances for the way a story gathers
as it goes from tongue to tongue. I think Lady
Dolly's estimate far more likely to be correct than
that circumstantial tale," and he pressed Geraldine's hand with warm friendliness as he saw the
blue eyes fill with tears even as she smiled farewell.

Geraldine threw herself back on the cushions
of her chariot, and rode on through the city a prey
to agonized doubt. These two months had been
full of anxiety, for there had been no cessation of

her father's pressure of Tarleton's suit, and that, together with the passionate love letters which Tarleton himself continued with clever ingenuity to have showered upon her (no matter how distant he might be), kept her in a perpetual state of excitement.   Margot was a great source of comfort to her young mistress during those trying days. Of course, all intercourse was forbidden between Rose and herself, but it was wonderful how little notes and words of cheer found their way to the plantation; sometimes from Cupid, who had been following his favorite occupation of bird-nesting and had met Rose in some mysterious manner; sometimes from Jumbo, to whom a missive had been delivered when exercising the horses.   And these had kept up Geraldine's heart, in a way, until Ossaba's interview with Rose had almost deprived her of hope.

But it was luxury to Geraldine to be alone, as the chariot rolled slowly along, for nowadays it seemed as if the long hours of the night were all she could claim as her own, and she had welcomed the opportunity to attend Lady Dolly's matinée because Colonel Moncriffe never rode to the city at that time unless called by official affairs.   Half the distance was passed, and she was nearing the plantation, when Jumbo's voice aroused her from her painful reverie : —

"Hole on dar ! what fer yo' do dat er way ? Don' yo' know, gal, dose hosses am 'fraid ob strange pussons ? " and wondering what could cause this excitement on Jumbo's part, Geraldine thrust her head through the window of the chariot as it drew up at the roadside, and saw, standing near the horses' heads, the picturesque form of Laceola.

Geraldine's first thought was of the strange beauty of the girl's face and form, as Laceola advanced slowly and with much dignity; her next, wonderment as to who the stranger might be.

"Laceola, the sister of Ossaba, would speak with the Pretty Tory," said the Indian girl; "will the daughter of the palefaces listen?"

"Laceola, the Indian girl whom Rose Telfair loves?" said Geraldine, her lovely smile lighting up the face that had been so sad; "will you come inside and sit beside me?"

Laceola smiled back at her, but coming close to the window she said softly, " The little room-on-wheels is too small to hold what Laceola would say. Will the Pretty Tory speak with Laceola beyond the thicket, there?" and she waved her hand toward a majestic oak which stood a few feet back from the roadside.

"Why do you call me the 'Pretty Tory'?" asked Geraldine as she sprang lightly out at the girl's bidding, and bade Jumbo wait until she returned.

" Dun like stoppin' hyar fur nuthin'," grumbled Jumbo; "lil missy not called fur to go round talkin' wif Injins an' sich wile cattle." But Geraldine had reached the tree, and the faithful black was forced to submit to the caprice of the young mistress whose dignity he so jealously desired to preserve.

"The paleface maiden is known as the 'Pretty Tory' in the settlement at Yamacraw because her father belongs to the soldiers of the king, but Laceola calls her the Maiden-with-hair-like-sunset. But listen, for the sun travels high, and Laceola must hasten away." She paused a moment, and then drew closer to Geraldine, who regarded her with eyes of pleased surprise. "Far away from here, beyond the Great River, there rides a brave young warrior; he goes to the camp of the Swamp Fox, but he must ride slowly, for his face is pale and his arm is weak. Lo! these two moons he lay ill with fever, and sorely wounded by the soldiers of the king."

Every vestige of color left Geraldine's face; she was white to the lips. "Roy — do you mean Roy?" she gasped.

"The Bounding Elk whose home is there." She pointed in the direction of Dumblane. "He bade Laceola come and bring tidings of his safety to his people, and" — she hesitated, and a blush came to her cheek — "Laceola knew that the Maiden-with-hair-like-sunset would rejoice."

With the sweet graciousness which became her so well Geraldine took the Indian girl's hand in hers. "Oh, thank God!" she cried, as the light came back to her eyes and the sunshine to her face, "he is not dead, as we heard."

"No, but for many days the Bounding Elk

knew nothing. But he was happy, for in his fever dreams he was wandering with the Pretty Tory whom he loves."

" Laccola!" Geraldine was trembling from head to foot; what did this child of the forest mean by probing her heart like this?

" Through the long night Laccola heard his prayers to the paleface maiden. She had listened kindly to the chief-who-loves-blood, and that hurt the Bounding Elk, and caused his heart to swell bitterly. What will the Pretty Tory do now, when both the chief-who-loves-blood and the Bounding Elk are again upon the warpath? which one will she select, and go to his wigwam?"

Geraldine threw back her haughty head, and her eyes gleamed like blue steel as she looked Laccola in the face.

" How dare you!" she said, scarcely above a whisper; " by what right do you question me upon my own most sacred affair?"

" Because Laccola loves the Bounding Elk," said the girl calmly; " she loves him far beyond herself. Her care, her hands, have brought him back to life almost from the spirit-land. Will the Pretty Tory make that life glad, or no?" Geraldine did not answer, and Laccola went on more rapidly: —

" The paleface maiden is proud, but she is no prouder than Laccola, in whose veins bounds the royal blood of an hundred chiefs who roamed these forests long before the soldiers of the king set foot in them. Why should Laceola give to any one the life she has saved? Because the Bounding Elk loves the maiden of his own race, and Laceola longs to see him smile again and be happy. Will the Pretty Tory make him so?"

The soft deep tones died trembling away as Laceola stood with bowed head and clasped hands. A wave of emotion shook Geraldine from head to foot; anger died almost as soon as born before the magnanimity, the self-abnegation of this untutored Indian girl. The love which elevated and ennobled her she sacrificed cheerfully and without a murmur, — her only wish, to see him happy. The thought pierced Geraldine's generous heart; she clasped Laceola in her arms and kissed her fondly.

"You have conquered," she said, her eyes full of tears. "My heart is his and his alone."

"But the rumor flies that the mansion at Glenmoira is being made ready for a bridal, and that the chief-who-loves-blood comes to wed the Pretty Tory."

"Never!" cried Geraldine passionately, and would have added more, but the Indian girl laid her hand on her lips.

"Some one rides up the road," she whispered; "Laceola must not be seen, for she risks capture as one of the Swamp Fox's scouts. There is a hollow tree near the summer-house on the plantation, and a paper placed there after sunset will reach the Bounding Elk. Farewell; lock up Laceola's secret and throw the key in the river of

forgetfulness," and pressing a kiss on the hand
she held, she ran swiftly into the thicket before
Geraldine could stay her flight.

Margot, after dressing her young mistress for
her ride to the city, and seeing her safely off under
Jumbo's care, tucked up her gown preparatory to
a grand cleaning raid which she felt it incumbent
upon her to inaugurate at unexpected intervals,
lest the blacks fall into untidy ways beyond her
control. At these seasons she was at once a terror
and inspiration to the entire household, even to the
smallest of the pickaninnies, who fled from her path
and sought refuge in the hedges until the fever of
"clarin' up" had subsided. But on this particular
occasion Margot proceeded no farther than the
kitchen door, for Colonel Moncriffe's gong was
sounding, and Phœbus appeared with eyeballs
rolling, to say that "marse wanted her in the
library immediately, ef not sooner."

"I wonder what's i' the wind?" said Margot to
herself, as she smoothed an almost imperceptible
wrinkle from her apron and hastened upstairs.
"There's been somewhat brewing for twa days
past, an' I dinna ken whose head will catch the
blast."

"Margot," remarked her master, as she walked
in, after a subdued rap, and closed the door behind her, "I have sent for you upon an important and rather confidential errand." Margot
courtesied. Colonel Moncriffe was turning over
papers on his desk, and kept his eyes carefully

"FAREWELL."

averted, as the shrewd old woman was quick to notice.

"I presume that you have understood from the fact of his visits and his close relations with the family that Colonel Tarleton is a suitor for the hand of my daughter. As the rebellion in the province keeps him perpetually upon the move, he is desirous of taking his bride as soon as the next victory permits of his going North to join the commander in chief, and from his last letter I am of the opinion that our arms will speedily be triumphant in the Carolinas. Therefore, within the coming month I feel assured that we may prepare for a wedding at Glenmoira, and have sent for you to inquire what amount of preparation will be necessary to make this the grandest event of its kind ever given in the province."

"A wedding!" said Margot in the most respectful of tones, but with a glint in her eye which boded no good to the speaker. "Weel, I 'm thinking, wi' due respect to your wishes, that it wad be mair harmonious for a' concerned if my young leddy gave her consent first."

"What do you mean, woman?" asked the colonel, falling back in his chair, and gazing at her with amazement and wrath plainly written on his countenance. "What do you know about my daughter's private affairs?"

"I ken mickle, an' I speir more. 'T is idle sparring between you an' me, sir; have I not been confidential maid to the mistress before even my young leddy was born, an' d' ye think Margot's eyes were blind all these years? I 've seen one life wither an' pass away because of your schemes an' wily ways, an' I promised the mistress on her dying bed that if ever I saw ye trying the same game wi' her child I 'd stop it, — an' the hour has come."

" What damned nonsense have you got into your head ? " cried the colonel, purple with rage. " Leave the room, and leave the house, for I will not submit to your insolence ! " Margot looked at him steadily, but he refused to meet her glance.

" It 's no for me to tell ye that my young leddy is near to break her heart wi' the pressure ye are bringing down on her, for ye ken yoursel' weel eno' the burden she has to bear frae your wrath an' the importunity of yon bloody Englishman. Why ye should be sae set on the marriage I hae bothered my brain, but I 'll think nae mair aboot it, for wi' due respect to ye, Colonel Moncriffe, without my young leddy's consent that marriage will ne'er tak place while Margot has words to speak an' breath to tell them."

" Your words, upon which you lay such ridiculous stress, have very little to do with the matter. Within a month my daughter weds Colonel Tarleton, and you will be packed back to Scotland."

" I 'm thankin' ye for my passage," said Margot coolly, " but bide a wee, an' hear what the auld wife has to say. So sure as ye persist in bringing doun despair an' unhappiness on Mistress Geraldine's bonnie head, Margot will keep your secret nae longer. How will it sound in the city — aye, an' across the water, where ye hold up your head sae high — if they find out how ye mak your money, an' the sin an' disgrace that sticks to ivery gold piece which passes through your fingers."

"My God!" The man sank back in his chair, huddled in a heap, trembling among the cushions, and regarded her with wide-open terror-stricken eyes. "How did you know — what am I saying? It's a foul lie, and your tongue should be torn out for uttering it."

"Ma tongue is safe eno'," said Margot firmly, "an' what I know, I *know*, an' I can give my testimony. But ye'll never come to that, sir; ye'll never let Margot tell how ye are a " —

"Stop!" shrieked the proud man, trying to rise, but unable to do so from absolute fright and agitation, "the walls have ears, woman. At least I can command you to hold your peace."

"Aye, sir," returned Margot, with an air of submission which completed her conquest. "I felt quite sure that ye wad never compel my young leddy to break her heart by wedding yon cruel monster (for the tales they tell o' him mak the hair raise on one's head), an' Margot has nae right to meddle save when her promise to the dead maun be keepit. I hae but done ma duty, sir, an' if ye please, wi' that clear in my mind an' a gude conscience, I'll gang doun and see that the blacks arrange the drawing-room wi' proper attention to cleanliness," and Margot dropped her lowest courtesy as she closed the door, a victor to the tips of her fingers.

CHAPTER XVIII

AT COWPENS

It was a bright, crisp January day, and in Marion's camp at Snow Island there was unusual activity even for that tireless command, for the famous partisan leader had returned with a body of his troopers, the evening before, from one of the expeditions which he had successfully planned against the British, having captured a wagon-train of ammunition which was joyfully welcome to the command.

Snow Island, Marion's favorite rendezvous, was a piece of high river swamp, as it is called in the Carolinas, and was surmounted on three sides by water, so as to be almost impregnable, and he rendered it even more so by destroying all bridges to the mainland, securing his boats carefully, and placing defenses where it was necessary. The island was a perfect labyrinth of paths, overgrown with vines and Southern vegetation, and almost impassable for one to traverse who was not familiar with its tortuous ways. The British had never been able to find it, even by aid of their Indian allies, and there the patriots found their one secure retreat either for rest, or for planning further action.

To Roy Telfair, this higher, purer air, and the life under the trees, was a veritable salvation after his long illness, and Marion, rejoiced at his rescue, for a long time forbade him any active service, beyond an occasional errand to the mainland. The gloom that had descended upon the patriots after the disastrous battle of Camden was dispelled by the spirited action at King's Mountain, and now the tide seemed to be upon the turn, as the regular troops had had a series of successful skirmishes in different localities since Morgan had come to the Carolinas and divided the army under General Greene. Tarleton had been detached with his newly recruited legion, now some eleven hundred strong, and was marching along the banks of the Pacolet, while Morgan with the American force was between the Catawba and the Black rivers, advancing with a rapidity unknown to the British commander.

This was the situation and these the tidings that Marion's scouts had brought, and even now the gallant partisan was debating whether to continue his harrying of the British or to proceed with the main body of his command to join Morgan on the Catawba. Being an irregular force of horse, composed chiefly of the militia of Georgia and the Carolinas, much was left (and wisely) to Marion's judgment and foresight in the matter of his military movements.

Roy Telfair was busily engaged in overlooking the condition of his horse (for which, since that

animal's gallant service, he had cherished the utmost regard), and came whistling along a shady
path on his way to more open ground when he
suddenly saw Colonel Marion advancing toward
him.

" Well met," said Marion, as the young officer
halted beside him. " I was coming to look for
you. Do you think you are able now for active
service ? "

" Both ready and eager, sir ; nothing could delight me more, for — though, thanks to your untiring care, I have enjoyed my return to health and
strength — I am absolutely pining to feel the saddle beneath me and be off."

" You shall have your wish," said Marion, smiling at the ready spirit which was so like his own.
" I am about to send dispatches to Colonel Morgan ; the service must be secret, and taken at once.
He is somewhere between the Black and the Catawba, but the scouts report him coming south-
westerly, and you will need to exercise great care,
for Tarleton is coming up to intercept him, and
there may be a battle."

" Nothing would please me more." A hot
sparkle rose in Roy's sunny eyes at the mention of
Tarleton's name. " When do I start, sir ? I am
ready."

" Then come with me," responded Marion, link-
ing his arm in Roy's, " and I will tell you what
the dispatches contain, lest by some mischance
you may have to destroy them to prevent their

falling into other hands than those for whom they are intended."

Some two hours after, Telfair, with his good horse, saddle-bags containing food and ammunition, and his dispatches safely hidden in his coat, was ferried by boat to the mainland, starting thus on the trail to find Morgan. McKay, somewhat envious of his friend's good fortune, but also rejoicing that he was so honored, accompanied him, and when the boat, paddled by Ossaba, drew in to the shore he stayed a moment to bid farewell.

"It hardly seems fair to separate us," he said with a regretful sigh, "but when I recollect the skeleton you were when you landed here, I am fain to thank kind Heaven that you can take the field again. Is there anything I can do for you here?"

"Nothing," answered Roy; and then as his glance fell on Ossaba, he stepped back and said softly, "only this. If aught befall me and I fail to report within reasonable time, contrive to send tidings of me by Ossaba."

"To Dumblane; aye, man, of course" —

"I had also said to Glenmoira," interposed Roy, a flush mounting to his bronzed cheek.

"Oh," returned McKay with a light laugh. "Have care, Telfair, the Pretty Tory is, they say, dangerously charming."

"I have always found her so; nay, McKay, 't is no new or light affair, but one for life, please God, though in these troublous times I care not to publish the matter," and lifting his hat in farewell

Roy rode away, leaving McKay divided between amazement and chagrin at his own stupidity.

Telfair's ride was not destined to be a very long one, but he spent the first night on the trail, finding it safer to travel under cover of darkness, and rest at noonday. He knew the country well, having ridden over a great part of it on previous raids, and he spared his horse all he could lest he should be called upon to press him for serious work.

Traveling thus steadily northward, Telfair came to the Pacolet River, and approached it warily, knowing that Tarleton could not be far distant. Searching for a ford was loss of time, and he rode carefully along the bank, intending to swim his horse across, when suddenly there rode into view from the thicket on his left two horsemen, who instead of dashing upon him, drew rein, and awaited his approach. With his hand on his pistol Roy rode straight for them, and as he came nearer his heart throbbed high, for the uniforms they wore were the brave old buff and blue.

"Halt, sir!" cried one of the officers, a tall, fine-looking man, who wore the rank of colonel, "from whence do ye come, and whither away?"

"I am at present in search of a spot to cross the river, sir, but I think I see before me those of the force I seek," returned Roy, saluting. "My name is Telfair, and I have the honor to bear a dispatch from Colonel Marion to General Morgan."

"Thrice welcome," said the first speaker, extending his hand with frank comradeship. "I am Colonel William Washington, commanding the cavalry corps attached to General Morgan's command, and am with my men (back there half a mile) about to join him as he has marched just ahead of me to Burn's Mills, on Thicketty Creek, a few miles farther north. You had better join us, as we take the shortest route we know, unless, perhaps, being a follower of the Swamp Fox, you may have greater knowledge of the locality than I can boast of."

"By no means, sir, although should you desire me to act as scout it will afford me the greatest pleasure to do so."

"I thank you, but we have several to act in that capacity, and Howard here," turning to the other officer with a laugh, "has an Indian girl who, he swears, for lightness of foot and keenness of vision has never been surpassed."

"And rarely equaled," returned Colonel Howard, of the Maryland brigade, as he bowed courteously to Telfair. "Since we chanced upon her two days ago, she has shrewdly pointed out several trails of value, and besides she carries safe-conduct signed by Colonel Marion."

"Laceola!" was Roy's surprised exclamation, and as he spoke her name the girl stepped out upon the bank from behind a willow tree, where she had remained concealed during this short colloquy.

"The Bounding Elk knows Laceola," she said, with smiling eyes of welcome; "she has scouted many a trail for him and the Rangers of the Swamp Fox."

" You 're well vouched for, my girl," said Washington, as Roy bent from his saddle and took Laccola's hand, " but we must not delay farther, as we have news that Tarleton is not far behind, and we must keep the force undivided. Your rank, sir, is — ah, captain ; then, Captain Telfair, we will follow your scout to the ford, which she tells us lies some quarter of a mile in yonder direction," and the three officers turned their horses and trotted briskly away.

Some forty miles in the rear of Colonel Washington's cavalry, marching rapidly to cross the Pacolet and prevent (as he supposed) Greene's reinforcements from joining Morgan, came Tarleton riding at the head of his column with Halleck in close conversation. Tarleton was in the highest spirits ; he had set an iron heel upon the Carolinas during the past three months, routing Sumter and proving successful in many small raids ; the only antagonist whom he could neither capture nor surprise being the wily and dashing Marion, and so sensitive was Tarleton upon this score that by common consent not an officer in his legion mentioned in his hearing the name of the redoubtable Swamp Fox.

" Tarleton," said Halleck, " Cornwallis seems to think this campaign will be prolonged into the spring, unless we can annihilate Morgan and force him into a position equivalent to being between the devil and the deep sea."

"In which I play the part of the devil," laughed Tarleton. "Well, the rôle suits me passing well. Cornwallis knows Morgan — he remembers Saratoga; see, here is his last letter to me," and putting his hand in the breast of his coat Tarleton drew forth the paper which he read aloud.

CAMP-IN-THE-FIELD, January 15.

DEAR TARLETON, — I sent Haldane to you last night, to desire you would pass the Broad River with the legion and the first battalion of the 71st as soon as possible. If Morgan is anywhere within your reach I should wish you to *push him to the utmost.* No time is to be lost.

Yours sincerely,

CORNWALLIS.[1]

"Short and to the point," said Halleck. "Faith, Tarleton, after this you can go back to seek your fair Geraldine in the character of a conquering hero."

Tarleton's face clouded, but he forced a laugh as he replied, "Oh, aye, but I own I aspire to be a conqueror in the court of love as much as in the field of war. Moncriffe writes that he is even now discussing the preparations for our wedding."

"I never expected to see you gaze with such calmness upon the forging of your fetters," laughed Halleck, who could seldom refrain from teasing his friend. But Tarleton would not pursue the subject, and after a moment resumed his

[1] See *Tarleton's Campaigns.*

discussion of the campaign as they rode rapidly on toward the river.

In the mean time, General Morgan, having received news that Tarleton was in close pursuit, halted his forces for one night only at Thicketty Creek, and by the time that Colonel Washington's column joined him, he was climbing a mountain road, and then striking a by-path, descended and encamped at Cowpens. Not until nightfall of that day did Roy Telfair obtain opportunity to deliver his dispatch, and when summoned, he found the general in council with his officers.

"From Colonel Marion, sir," said Roy, as he saluted and fell back, rejoiced at the chance thus afforded to meet the hero of many battles, and one of the most strikingly handsome men of the times. Standing over six feet, with magnificent physique, an eye keen as an eagle's, a smile kindly as a woman's, Morgan was a leader calculated to inspire enthusiasm and devotion. He read the dispatch, and beckoned Roy to approach.

"I thank you, sir, for your speed, but the fortunes of war compelled me to bring you hither. Colonel Marion's offer of bringing his command to join me is fully appreciated, but at present I cannot order him to do so. We must meet the enemy to-morrow with what force I have, and God defend the cause of freedom!" He paused a moment, glanced around the circle, and again addressed Roy.

"Do you prefer to return, or to stop with me

on the eve of a battle? Aye,"—he smiled as
Roy's answer was written on his eloquent face,—
"I thought it would be so; young blood ever
warms at the clash of arms, and my own has not
yet grown too old to do the same. I can give you
a staff appointment for the time being. Washington, what say you to a recruit from Marion's
forces?"

"With great pleasure, general," replied Colonel Washington. "I could not ask a better aide-
de-camp than Captain Telfair."

"So be it; you have hard work before you, sir,
and plenty of it. We all know Tarleton; what's
that?" as loud cheers were heard on the right.

"Colonel Pickens, general, who has crossed the
Broad River and brings with him an hundred and
fifty men," said an officer, springing from his
horse, and extending his hand to Morgan. But
the general threw his arms around him, and fairly
hugged the gallant Pickens in his delight at seeing
him.

There was little sleep in the American camp
that night, and for Morgan there was no repose.
Company after company of militia poured in, all
eager to join the "Border Eagle" in the coming
fight, and no one knew better than he how to
mould together the homogeneous material. His
very presence inspired them with confidence; his
dignity and courage, with his fame as a leader who
had never met defeat, combined to fill that little
army of eight hundred with the wildest enthusiasm,

and by the time morning dawned over the field of Cowpens every man was burning for the fight, sure that success depended upon his individual prowess.

It was not more than three o'clock in the morning when an advance guard of Tarleton's cavalry drove one of Morgan's patrols into camp, and the general, who had been endeavoring to snatch a few minutes' rest, began at once to post his detachments. After the militia were placed, came the regulars, and Roy found himself upon a slight eminence, about a hundred and fifty yards in the rear of the main body, with Colonel Washington and his cavalry as a support to the militia, and back of them were the extra horses, saddled and bridled for any emergency.

Roy, sent for a moment by Colonel Washington to see if the horses were properly secured and attended, went on foot to execute the errand, and as he stood inspecting the position, in the early dawn, he heard the low sound of a voice proceeding from some underbrush near him, and stepped aside to see who and what it was. Peering through the bushes, what was his surprise to see the giant form of Morgan kneeling on the grass, and to overhear his supplication : —

" Thou knewest, O Lord, that I shall be very busy this day ; if I forget Thee, do not Thou forget me, nor Thy sacred cause of Freedom and Liberty with which Thou hast imbued the souls of our people. They say that Morgan never fears, they

say that Morgan never prays, but Thou knowest,
O Lord, that he is terribly afraid at times, and
that he prays to-day that he may have courage to
smite the enemy hip and thigh, to Thy Eternal
glory, Amen ! " [1]

As softly as he came, Roy sped away, his heart
swelling as he thought that nothing could ever con-
quer a people who prayed as fervently as they
fought.

And that day, as always, the little band of devoted patriots fought nobly, fought with a dogged
determination, a desperate coolness, which made
the battle of Cowpens the decisive combat of the
South, and its results far-reaching in the war of
independence. From the moment when Tarleton
himself led the opening attack to the time when
the militia, mistaking an order, retreated, breaking
their lines (and deceiving the British thereby,
who imagined a victory was achieved), the combat
went on with glory for the American arms. But
what seemed a calamity was turned into a victory
by the splendid military genius of Morgan and
Howard, and as Howard's main line ascended the
second eminence the word " Halt " was given. A
moment's pause, and Morgan's grand voice rang
down the hill : —

" Face about, one good fire, and the victory is
ours ! "

On rushed the Marylanders ; Lee with his famous Virginia horsemen were on the height, and

---

[1] See Graham's *Life of Morgan*.

Washington in the rear thundered as he rose in his stirrups, " *Charge!* "   Before that glorious onslaught the British lines wavered, and then went down, and lay, conquered, at the feet of the patriots.

" Come on," shouted Washington to Roy Telfair, as they saw a handful of the 17th Dragoons headed by Tarleton himself, who essayed to rally his men ; but finding his efforts vain, the British commander turned to flee.   Nothing loath, Roy dashed ahead, distancing even Washington himself in his wild eagerness to cross swords again with Tarleton, this time on equal terms.   Tarleton, turning in his saddle, saw the two, and drew his rein.

" To the rescue, Halleck," he shouted, and, wheeling as he spoke, met Roy's sabre-stroke with another equally fierce, while Halleck crossed swords with Washington.   Suddenly Washington's sword, being of inferior steel, broke near the hilt, and Halleck rose in his stirrups to give a final blow to Telfair, who was pressing Tarleton hard.   But before either British officer could accomplish his purpose, a slight form rose from the ground, a pistol shot rang in the air and Halleck's uplifted sword fell from his hand, to be grasped by Colonel Washington, who turned upon Tarleton with the utmost fury, as Laceola staggered back, struck by a passing bullet.   Up dashed the troopers to Washington's aid, and the pursuit of Tarleton across the field began.   But as he saw the flight of his enemy, Roy sprang from his saddle, and lifted the Indian girl from the spot where she had fallen.

" Laceola ! " he cried. " Oh, my God, are you wounded ? " Laceola opened her dark eyes; a flood of light beamed in their beautiful depths as she smiled up in the anxious face above her.

" It is nothing," she said softly : " the Bounding Elk must not grieve," and then she lay senseless in his arms.

CHAPTER XIX

WHO WINS?

FROM the disastrous field of Cowpens, stunned
with its surprises, filled with rage at his defeat
by a force three hundred less than his own,
Tarleton fled with unequaled rapidity, pursued by
Washington and his cavalry for twenty miles.   He
had managed to secure Halleck's bridle-rein, and
with the devotion that he frequently displayed
toward his friends, contrived to have a trooper take
special charge of his wounded comrade, and conduct him aside from the main trail where he could
find aid and succor, while he kept the Americans
still in pursuit of himself and his handful of the
17th Dragoons, and reached at last the bank of
the Broad River, from whence he could easily com-
municate with Cornwallis at Winsborough Court
House.   And there, the Americans having turned
back to rejoin Morgan, Tarleton remained over a
day and night, to endeavor to recover from his
chagrin, and send dispatches to his superior officer.
The slight wound which he had received from
Washington burned with consuming fire, and his
haughty spirit could ill brook the humiliation of
being worsted, with Roy Telfair as witness of his
discomfiture.

Bivouacking thus, on the farther bank of the river, Tarleton was reached and found the next day by Burt, who, having passed the trooper sent to report to Cornwallis, obtained from him tidings of Tarleton's whereabouts, and was thus able to fetch before his commander the scout who brought a return message from headquarters.

"Burt," called Tarleton, some half hour later, during which the British officer had been pacing hastily up and down the narrow limits of his bivouac, "are you ready to start again?"

"Aye, sir; after my horse is fed; he is at present taking a much needed meal."

"I go forward at daybreak," said Tarleton, "and join Lord Cornwallis for special conference. But I wish to dispatch you southward with all speed. I have written two letters," pulling the somewhat soiled papers from his breast as he spoke; "they are, as you see, for Mistress Moncriffe and her father. You will ride dispatch from here, crossing the Edisto at the point where a detachment of our troops are watching Marion's movements, and thence to Savannah. I shall probably follow you shortly, and send you in advance to announce my presence at Glenmoira. Keep a silent tongue to all outside the plantation as to my anticipated trip; if you need money, apply to the commandant at Fort Wayne. That is all," and turning moodily away Tarleton resumed his restless walk to and fro.

The fourth day after Burt started upon his

errand he drew rein, as he walked his somewhat
tired horse slowly down the main street of the little village of Ebenezer.   Not only was the German
settlement his shortest route, but he knew he could
obtain a fresh mount from the British garrison
there, and moreover he had a commission of his
own to execute.   As he drew near the door of the
smithy, he saw within Wilhelm himself, at work
at his anvil.

"Good-day, friend," called Burt, as the blacksmith paused, hearing the sound of horse's hoofs.
"'T is some months since we met, but I trust I
shall not have to recall myself to your memory
after the manner of last time;" and he laughed at
the recollection, as Wilhelm came forth with
hearty welcome.

"What news to-day?" asked the German, having shaken hands lustily.   "Art the bringer of
good tidings?"

"That depends much upon to whom I am speaking," returned Burt with a shrewd twinkle of his
eye.   "Last time I shocked your ears and my own
with the account of the massacre at Waxhaw; to-
day I bring news of a terrible defeat at Cowpens" —

"Alas, alas!" groaned the smith.

"Nay, man, you are in too great haste, and did
not hear all my news.   What do you say to Tarleton's forces being crushed — aye, almost wiped
out, with the prisoners counted in — by General
Daniel Morgan of the Continental Army, and
Tarleton himself put to flight with a handful of
troopers, of which I am one."

"Huzza!" cried the smith, seizing his hat and flinging it so high in the air that it caught on a bough of the tree under which they stood, and dangled there just out of his reach. Burt laughed, and the German surveyed his exploit with a rather sheepish air, but he said, "The news is worth my old hat; what will the garrison yonder say to it?"

"I shall proceed to condole with them," replied Burt dryly. "But what I paused for was to ascertain how fell out our little affair which was so ably planned to secure the fort at Savannah?"

"We could not work it; when you left the train was well laid, but it required more men than the Swamp Fox could well spare at the time, as he was sent for to go to a place where a battle was fought."

"That was Camden, and a fine fool's errand Gates sent Marion upon that time! Well, 't was a good scheme, that of ours, and one I spent much time and trouble over, but it was not to be for all my pains. I must be off, so fare you well."

The Cherokee roses were beginning to bud and blossom in the hedges at Glenmoira some ten days later, and the softest air and sunshine greeted Tarleton as he rode up the avenue in his most carefully appointed fashion. Obtaining a brief leave from Cornwallis, and combining with an elaborately planned military movement his own intended marriage, he had arrived at Savannah the day previous, and putting up at the fort, was the guest of Colonel Prevost. He had expected no reply to his letters announcing his speedy arrival, and he grew more and more impatient as he came nearer the scene of his anticipated conquest. For Tarleton had determined that he would be patient no longer, but press his wooing to a triumphant conclusion.

In the door of the mansion stood Jupiter, drawn thither by the sound of the horse's feet, and he came down the steps with due deliberation, in his heart most devoutly wishing that the " raidcoat colonel " was where he came from.

" Yo' servant, sir," he began, bowing, and Jupiter's bow was a study, and always graduated in proportion to his regard. " Marse Colonel has not entirely made his toilet dis mornin', but yo' mus' 'cuse him, sar, 'caise he dun know de honah you 'se payin' him."

" Jupiter, you old rascal," shouted the voice of Colonel Moncriffe as he appeared in the door just in time to hear this apology, " take that horse around and be quick about it," and he grasped Tarleton's hand with a cringing air most foreign to his usual pompous manner.

" You had my letters," said Tarleton, following his host inside the mansion, as Moncriffe led the way to the library. " I hope that every arrangement is made for my speedy bridal, as 't is only by great pressure that I am able to absent myself from the field, as most important military opera-

tions in the Carolinas demand my return almost
immediately. How and where is my fair bride?"

"She is well," stammered Moncriffe, as Tarleton flung himself into a chair and looked him im-
patiently in the face. "I would that your whereabouts had been known, for I wished to answer
your favor sent by Burt."

"And wherefore, sir? Surely there had been
time enough for preparation? There is a limit to
my patience," and a fiery spark lit in Tarleton's
dark eyes.

"I — I — cannot — in short, sir, deeply as I
regret to say it, I find that although I would willingly bestow my daughter's hand upon you, she
still refuses her consent to go with you to the
altar."

"By God! sir," cried Tarleton, hot with anger,
"was not our little arrangement made with due
attention to detail? Must I rehearse its provisions again? In consideration of my silence in regard to your nefarious operations extending over
some years, during which you have repeatedly and
by stealth sold into slavery hundreds of negroes
employed by the government, and pocketed the
proceeds, amounting to thousands of pounds," —

"Hold!" murmured the miserable man; "you
need not repeat it" —

— "In addition to this crime, which places you
within the power of the law, you deliberately falsified
my accounts six months ago, — the paper falling
into my hands, and" —

"You told me it was destroyed," faltered Moncriffe. "Oh, spare me" —

"I hold you to the terms of our compact: your daughter's hand, sir, or I publish to the world your private career. You have held high estate too long for such villainies; 't will afford a fine scandal for investigation in the military affairs of this province."

Moncriffe clutched the table near which he stood to save himself from falling, as a rap sounded softly on the door of the room, and Margot appeared upon the threshold.

"If ye please, sir," she said, respectfully addressing Colonel Moncriffe, "my young leddy is waiting to see Colonel Tarleton in the drawing-room."

"I follow you," said Tarleton, rising, and smoothing his countenance as if by magic, he left the room without a glance at its miserable master, who sank trembling into the nearest chair.

Geraldine rose from her seat in a high-backed carved chair as Tarleton entered, and never had she seemed more beautiful or more stately to his passionate, admiring gaze. The sunshine from the open window played and flickered over her wonderful ruddy hair and lost itself in the folds of her white gown as she gave him her hand with her own peculiar grace.

"I sent for you, Colonel Tarleton," she said, as he, in almost involuntary homage, threw himself on one knee before her, "because I wish to spare my father the pain that I am aware my present action will cause him. Had I only known how a dispatch could reach you I should not have allowed you to come upon this bootless errand. My letters must have prepared you for this avowal; I have never felt for you one particle of affection, and unless my heart goes with my hand I will never bestow either upon mortal man."

Tarleton sprang to his feet. "Can nothing move you?" he cried. "Geraldine, I adore you with a love far exceeding your wildest imagination. Many, many times have I uttered vows of devotion, but they came only from my lips — they were but the passing emotion of the hour, caused by the senses; they died the death of ephemeral passion, and like the whirlwind vanished into air. Your purity, your calm serenity, is to me like a draught of water to a dying man. Your beauty, while it fires my imagination, fills me with awe lest by a word too much I brush the delicate bloom off your innocent cheek. Doom me not to despair, for I swear to you that unless I can possess you no other woman shall ever be led to the altar by Banastre Tarleton."

Well was it said of Tarleton that he knew how to sway the human heart, and to do him justice, for the first and only time in his career he was sincere in his masterly effort to attain his purpose. No woman could have been insensible to his seductive voice and manner, and Geraldine's noble and generous nature was moved almost to the point of surrender.

"Sir," she said, and her sweet voice trembled, "if there were but one spark of affection, however dim, in my breast for you, your words would light the flame. I cannot but feel that I have been in fault in allowing my father and you to persuade me to give you false hopes, and for that I crave your forgiveness. And perhaps I am all the more culpable in my own eyes "— a burning, beautiful blush dyed her face — "because I feel it my duty to confess that for years another has filled my heart beyond hope of change."

"And that other," cried Tarleton, rage taking violent possession of him, "that other is — nay, madam, you do not need to speak his name — a rebel, in arms against your king; whose life, in a moment of foolish generosity, I spared at your request."

Geraldine surveyed him for an instant in silence. "If my recollection serves, Captain Telfair spared *you*, — at his sword's point, — and moreover, sir, my gratitude to you in that matter is somewhat obscured by the knowledge that while promising me that your prisoner's life was accorded him, you sent secret advices to Colonel Prevost which, had not Captain Telfair fortunately made his escape, would have resulted in his being shot upon arrival at the fort. I think, sir, that it were well to omit both generosity and gratitude in your account of the matter and to bring this interview to a close."

Tarleton stood transfixed as her scornful words lashed him. How had she ever learned that secret which he thought buried in his own breast? But as he started forward to detain her, the door opened and Colonel Moncriffe entered.

"Geraldine, my child," he began, "I have come to add my persuasions" —

"Pray spare yourself the exertion." Tarleton's sneer was deadly in its significance. "I do not now care to enter the family of a man whom I know to be" — the words were frozen on his lips, for with an awful cry which rang through the house, Moncriffe fell forward at Geraldine's feet, dead before he touched the floor.

CHAPTER XX

THE REBEL BLUE

" I DO by no means agree with you," said Lady Dolly decidedly; " the palest shade of lavender by all means, and if you must have a dash of blue to do honor to the occasion, wear it as a breast-knot. 'T will be a delicate compliment in more ways than one," and the fair, but mischievous dame leaned back in her chair and regarded Geraldine with eyes that twinkled with enjoyment.

There was bustle and hurry in the streets of Savannah, and in the offing lay a score of vessels, making ready to sail as the sun set over a new and ransomed province. For in the eighteen months since the star of victory shone over Cowpens, there had been little pause in the march of events which freed Georgia and the Carolinas from the cruel despotism of Cornwallis and Tarleton, and crowned with triumph the patriots of the South when the American forces met at Yorktown.

But although not enough troopers to form a corporal's guard were left in the sister provinces after the conflict at Eutaw Springs (of which Fox said in the House of Commons "another such

victory would ruin the British army "), the British
still continued to hold with unrelenting grasp the
cities of Savannah and Charleston, and Roy Telfair was still with his beloved leader Marion, and
had escaped unhurt from many a skirmish with
his implacable foe, Tarleton, who, commanding at
Gloucester when Cornwallis surrendered his army
at Yorktown, was compelled to take refuge under
the protection of the French general, Choisé,
because he dared not fall into the hands of the
American militia, and had gotten safely away to
England, where he was rewarded for his services
to the crown by being sent to Parliament and
created a baronet. But after he set sail a letter
came by private hand to Geraldine.

On Board H. M. Ship Hornet.

Lovely and Beloved Mistress (it ran),
—When these Lines are read by Eyes more beautiful than the Sea, more witching than those of
Argive Helen, thy wretched Tarleton will be far
away never to return to These pestilent Shores.
Would that my Pen were a quill of the fabled
Swan that it might Sing thy Praises and my Despair! For while I Threatened I Adored, and I
think of Thee in sorrow and alone, and Curse fate
who Separates us. Oh, Mistress of Tarleton's
heart, deign Sometimes to drop a tear such as may
wet the Eye of Purity for even the most miserable of mankind, and as it falls Remember him
who while Life lasts will gain his only glimpse of

Heaven as his sad Eyes dwell upon the pictured Face of Her whom he leaves, and leaving, still Adores. Thy lover,

BANASTRE TARLETON.

Geraldine laid the letter down with a throb of pity for the strange contradictions which went to make up a character at once fascinating and repulsive, ungoverned, yet at times restrained and always of meteor-like brilliancy. And through a life prolonged beyond the years of most men, Tarleton kept faith with his American love, for when he died, a solitary recluse, there hung beside his bed, where his last look could rest upon it, a miniature, on the back of which in faded writing was inscribed " The Fair Geraldine."

When the tragedy of Colonel Moncriffe's death had shocked all Savannah, the first to come to Geraldine were Rose and Madam Telfair, and then Lady Dolly, whose madcap brain was balanced by her warm heart, and when after the funeral, she ventured to suggest that perhaps her presence at Glenmoira might be of use, Geraldine caught eagerly at the idea and begged her to stay on the plantation. For Lady Dolly was in no way connected with any thought which gave pain to her young hostess, and her tact and good taste soon made her a reigning favorite at Glenmoira, for, as Margot shrewdly observed, " Her Ladyship was na precisely ane thing or t'ither, being a gude Tory wi' fine Whig principles."

So, to-day, as the friends sat in Geraldine's morning room, the point under discussion was the ceremony which was to be enacted at sunset in Savannah, for the British general, Clarke, had concluded his negotiations with General Wayne for the surrender of the city to the American forces, and the keys were to be delivered by the British commander at the principal gate, where the formal surrender would take place in the presence of both British and American soldiers and the entire population of Savannah. Major Habersham, an officer of the Georgia legion and a distinguished patriot, had invited the Telfairs and Geraldine to witness the surrender of the keys, and as Lady Dolly vowed she could not see the ceremony, she was to be left at the plantation to await Geraldine's return.

Geraldine was standing beside her bed, contemplating two gowns which were laid there for her inspection by Margot, who stood listening respectfully while the discussion went on. Geraldine inclined to the white, Lady Dolly to the lavender, and finally Margot fastened the soft clinging stuff around her young mistress' graceful form and stood back, while Geraldine surveyed herself in the mirror and blushed like a rose at her own beauty.

"Aye," quoth Lady Dolly, holding her at arms' length, "you have found your colors at last. Strange how the wheel of fortune turns. I wonder who will take part in the procession to-day?"

"How can I tell?" answered Geraldine, as Margot fetched the big hat with its white plumes, which gave the added touch of the picturesque to her charming toilet. "Oh, Margot, hasten; I hear the wheels; that must be the Telfairs' chariot. I did not know they meant to come for me; tell Jumbo to follow us closely, for I must return with him. I do not wish to fetch Rose so far out of her way again," and with a kiss and a smile Geraldine said farewell to Lady Dolly and sped away down the staircase.

Seated in the chariot, drawn by two fine bays, was Madam Telfair. Rose, she explained, had gone into the city at an earlier hour with her father, and then Madam Telfair checked her speech suddenly; there was one piece of news which she had been carefully warned not to carry to Geraldine.

The city was in gala dress, but in what unwonted colors! From every house as they drove slowly along (for the crowd filled the sidewalks and overflowed into the roadway) the buff and the blue floated joyously, and at last the horses drew up a few hundred yards from the city gate. Out on the bay the little white-capped waves tossed and played, the fort stood silent and grim in the sunshine, and on shore, lined up, were the garrison, their scarlet coats making a brilliant bit of color in the picture upon which Geraldine gazed with quickening breath and wide, shining eyes. Every one she knew was in that long line of chariots and foot passengers, and presently outside the town came the long, sweet notes of the bugles which told that the patrols were approaching.

Leaning back in the chariot, far down the line, sat Rose Telfair, but though her heart beat high with joy, there was an undertone which, disdain as she would, caused her to bite her lips and turn aside as she recognized in the crowd just beyond the Durbeville girls, and saw a figure she knew well pause to speak to them. Truly, it was hardly becoming that Allastar Murray should even be present at this ceremony; she was glad, of course, that he had come to his senses sufficiently to understand that she could have naught to do with a swain who retained his Tory principles, but surely Molly Durbeville was not — And then Rose's reflections came to a sudden and speedy end, for a hand was laid on the sill of the window close by hers and a voice she had longed to hear said, —

" Have you no word of farewell for me, sweet cousin ? I sought you at Dumblane this morning, but you had left for the city."

" Farewell ! " echoed Rose, with a start, as she met the eyes regarding her so closely, " surely ; and a pleasant voyage to you. When do you sail ? "

" Sir James has preceded me to New York and keeps passage for me there, because " —

" Because you cannot quite make up your mind whether you prefer old England to our newer, freer life in the provinces," said Rose, with curling lip ; why did something rise in her throat and swell up in her eyes? She dropped them as she spoke, and to her infinite chagrin a bright tear escaped between the long lashes, and fell glittering on the hand which lay, big and brown, on the window-sill.

"Rose," — the bugles were sounding nearer and nearer, and every head was turned toward the approaching music, — "little Whig and rebel that you are, do you not know that one word from you will make me stay, aye, even in a far less attractive land and life than this which you have taught me to love?"

Rose caught her breath, and Allastar Murray bent his head almost to the pretty cheek as she granted his request in her own sweet fashion. "Stay — and see our troops come in. I will even make room for you in the chariot." Then, as he hesitated, half afraid to believe his own good fortune, "Stay, unless you would break my heart," said she.

Outside the gate came the tramp of horses' feet, and in the open, as the troops parted to admit the Americans, stood General Clarke, keys in hand. At the head of the incoming column rode Colonel Jackson, who had been delegated by General Wayne to receive the surrender, and as the horsemen passed each other hat in hand, there rang out from the shore the deep-mouthed bay of the cannon in the salute of thirteen guns. Down from the flagstaff on the fort fluttered the English ensign, and in its place there floated over a free

city freedom's own banner, — the Stars and Stripes
of the United States.

Cheer upon cheer greeted the little band of regulars as they swung along, but when to the eyes
of the delighted crowd there came — his famous
Indian scouts Ossaba and Laceola, leading the
way with their free proud step — a small, but con-
spicuous figure, followed by the well-known and
well-beloved Rangers, a shout fairly rent the air
of "Marion! Marion!" as the gallant partisan,
bending to his saddle-bow, rode along, compelled
to halt for the hands stretched out to clasp his
and the blessings that were invoked by every voice
upon the Defender of the South.

Geraldine, her hands clasped, the swift blood
surging to and fro in her lovely face, maintained
her composure until she caught sight of Laceola,
as the Indian girl led the Rangers. Then an over-
powering timidity seized her, and seeing that
Madam Telfair was bending forward, all intent
upon the pageant, Geraldine quickly opened the
door of the chariot, and fled, absolutely fled, a few
steps behind, where she knew Jumbo was waiting
for his mistress. Without pausing for reflection
she sprang into the chariot, and crouching low
among the cushions, gave the order to the surprised and much disappointed Jumbo : —

"Home! take the back streets and hasten
quickly."

There was that in her tone which made the
black obey, and in a few minutes Geraldine found

herself, dizzy and panting from the terror of her newborn emotions, rolling along as rapidly as the horses could carry her, while behind her came the shouts and booming guns of a rejoicing people. But just as they turned into the avenue at Glenmoira the reaction came ; how could she be so ungracious, — so unloving, — what would Roy think, — Roy, whom she had not seen since that never to be forgotten night in the governor's garden, when she had learned that all the heart she had was his ; — and to flee from him thus. Oh, surely she had been mad ; and she wrung her hands in dismay as she wondered what spirit of perversity had possessed her.

The horses halted before the door, but as Geraldine sprang from the chariot her quick ear caught the sound of ringing hoof beats as they came tearing up the avenue in pursuit, and before she could collect her bewildered senses sufficiently to assume the dignified and proper demeanor befitting the occasion, the reins were flung on the neck of the panting horse, and Roy's dear merry eyes were gazing into hers, and his triumphant voice ringing in her ear, —

" Traitress — to flout me thus ! Nay, just one kiss to bid me welcome to my own."

And so Margot and Lady Dolly found them, and Geraldine was fain to forget her dignity, and submit to be led up the staircase by this lordly young lover, who gave her no time to abdicate from her woman's throne.

Two days after there was a grand dinner at
Glenmoira, which no untoward incident interrupted, where Marion himself graced the board,
where toasts and speeches were the order of the
hour, and the health of the " Blue Bell of Scotland" was drunk with three times three, and
where Roy Telfair, radiant young bridegroom,
toasted his bride, in teasing, playful fashion, with
a rhyme which has come down, losing none of its
quaint flavor, to this generation : —

> "Say, pretty Tory, coy as fair,
> Of the King's colors be you ware,
> When in those eyes of heaven's own hue,
> Reluctant smiles the Rebel blue !'"